THE SOCIAL SHIFT:
THE ROAD BACK TO COMMUNITY

BY KATIE BRINKLEY

"If you need a comprehensive overview of social media for marketing and community building, look no further. Katie Brinkley has done all of us a great service by providing a historical (did you know the telegram is the historical grandfather to social media?) and philosophical view of how each platform emerged. But don't get too lost in the history—the gold lies in chapter 8 where she shared her unique four-post strategy. This is an easy read laced with personal stories and industry examples. I'll be referencing it as I grow my side hustle."

—Phil Mershon, Director of Experience for Social Media Examiner

"Have you noticed how social media feels more like a shopping mall and less like a friendly gathering these days? You're not alone. Katie Brinkley's book, The Social Shift, is all about that change. She dives deep into how we went from cozy chats online to being swamped by ads. But Katie's genius lies not just in her brilliant observations but in her actionable solutions. She gives a sneak peek into future tech, how to ride its wave, and, most importantly, how to bring back that genuine human touch to our digital interactions. If there's one guide to navigating and rejuvenating the social media landscape, this is it. A must-read filled with wisdom and heart!"

—Jeff Sieh, Host of Social Media News Live

"Katie's book is the perfect deep dive into how we can transform social media back into something real. She really nails how far we've gotten from those early days when it was all about bringing people together. But Katie doesn't just look back—she gives us a roadmap to the future where human connections shine again. Her advice for being genuine and using tech to revive relationships is so on point. Whether you're getting your business out there or just trying to connect, this book will inspire you to be the awesome positive force we need online. Katie's wisdom helps me stay true to my mission of making authentic connections and spreading joy. If you wanna breathe life back into social media, you gotta get into this!"

—Molly Mahoney, Founder of The Prepared Performer

Dedication

───────

This book is lovingly dedicated first and foremost to my family—my constant foundation. Your unwavering love and support have nurtured me throughout this journey and all my pursuits. Thank you for shaping me into the person I am today. I would not be where I am without you.

I also dedicate this book to the mentors who have guided me along the way. Your wisdom and encouragement have been invaluable in shaping my professional path. By generously sharing your insights, you've helped unlock my potential and equipped me for new horizons.

Finally, this book is dedicated to the pioneers of social technology who sparked a communications revolution bringing our world closer together. Your innovations laid the groundwork for the vibrant virtual communities we now enjoy.

In particular, I dedicate this to Tom from MySpace, a true pioneer of social connection. At a time when digital friendships seemed a far-fetched idea, you opened our eyes to the power of social media. You taught us the internet could be more than just a repository of information—it could be a bridge between people. Your legacy lives on each time we virtually "friend" someone new. Thank you for being a catalyst of the connected generation.

CONTENTS

Foreword

———————

In 2007, I made a bold decision. I left my executive position at one of North America's largest publishing companies to embark on an entrepreneurial journey. To many, it seemed like a crazy move. I had limited startup capital and a seemingly far-fetched idea that had no guarantee of success.

However, I possessed a secret weapon that most people either weren't using or didn't fully comprehend: social media.

I plunged headfirst into platforms like Twitter (now X) and LinkedIn. Through a mix of posting and sharing strategies, I rapidly gathered over 100,000 followers on each platform. These followers not only engaged with my content but also tuned in to my podcasts, subscribed to my blog, and attended our annual conference. In under a decade, our company had grown into a $10 million success story.

A substantial share of the credit went to the power of social media.

Social media became the backbone of a thriving community. I forged connections with individuals that would have been unimaginable in previous years. Many of those connections remain cherished friends to this day.

But, regrettably, the rules of the game have evolved.

The algorithms that once facilitated genuine connections and community-building have become obsolete. In their place, we find millions of users endlessly scrolling, sharing memes, and spending hours on platforms like Instagram and TikTok, all while lacking meaningful engagement.

The strategies that brought us success with social media years ago are no longer effective.

This book you're holding or viewing on your tablet is a crucial part of the new strategy. Katie's book embarks on a journey that reevaluates the origins of social media and prompts us to consider how we can rediscover authentic relationships and purposeful communication in this rapidly changing landscape.

She encourages us to reflect on whether, as social media continues its breakneck evolution, we are deepening our connections with others or simply getting lost in the whirlwind of the digital rat race.

I still firmly believe that social media can be a force for good, both for us as individuals and as business owners. However, we must first acknowledge that our current approach to social media isn't working and then develop a new plan that aligns with the demands of this next era of social media.

Enjoy this book as the beginning of a better way.

Yours in Content

Joe Pulizzi

Founder, The Tilt and Author, Content Inc.
and Epic Content Marketing

Preface

———

"Community." That's a word that seems to carry a different weight for each of us, doesn't it? Yet it's something we all yearn for, both physically and virtually. I, too, am on a perpetual quest for community—a product of being a "geriatric millennial," a term I've gradually come to embrace.

You see, I'm an "old" millennial, a pioneer of sorts who has grown up alongside the blossoming internet. The architects behind the platforms we know and love (and sometimes love to hate) aren't much older, or younger, than me. This puts me in a unique position—a bridge between two worlds, the analog and the digital.

Before the dark clouds of online bullying shadowed the social networking landscape, I roamed these halls freely. My concerns were limited to passing paper notes in the hallways between classes and hoping the recipient would perceive the careful intent behind my words. In a way, these formative experiences have shaped how I view and interact with the digital world, which is something I want to pass on to my children.

As a mother of two wonderful young girls, I'm already experiencing the digital age dilemma. "Mom, when can I get a phone?" This innocent question struck a chord, reminding me of the two-sided coin that is technology. Sure, I got my first phone as a junior in high school, a fact that did little to impress my impatient daughters. But we all know the times have changed.

Despite my own fond memories of the pre-digital age, I am keenly aware that denying my children their digital tools in a world so vastly interconnected would be doing them a disservice. Their journey into the world of smartphones will undoubtedly begin before their high school years.

And yet as I consider this inevitability, a seed of apprehension takes root. The moment they have those devices in their hands, they'll join the ranks of countless other kids diving headfirst into social media networks, messaging apps, and photo-sharing sites. I can almost see their afternoons, once filled with carefree play and giggles, consumed by texting friends and watching videos on those tiny screens. My biggest fear? Losing them to their online friends, their virtual community.

While grappling with these parental worries, I can't help but remember my own journey into the digital landscape. It began innocently enough, with the playful tinkering of MySpace in my college days. That's right—I've been part of the social media revolution since its inception.

You could say that I've grown up alongside these platforms, experienced their teething problems and milestones, much like a watchful elder sibling. It's this deep-seated familiarity that has allowed me to navigate the murky waters of the digital world with a certain deftness.

But let me rewind a bit—I'm Katie Brinkley, a self-professed geriatric millennial with an unwavering passion for social media and its untapped potential. I've journeyed from being a budding radio broadcaster in Denver, Colorado, navigating my way through sports commentaries, to realizing my true calling lay elsewhere—in the boundless realm of marketing.

It's not just my professional detour into marketing that shaped my understanding of social media, though. It's also the lessons I've learned as a parent, trying to prepare my children for their digital future. This mix of personal and professional experiences has shown me that the world of social media, as complex and chaotic as it may be, is also a realm brimming with possibilities. It's a landscape where meaningful connections can be forged and vibrant communities can flourish.

Despite its challenges, I've come to appreciate the beauty of this digital ecosystem. And as I've evolved along with it, I've discovered new terrains that reinforce my belief in the power of community—the worlds of podcasting, Web3, and NFTs.

Equipped with my knowledge of and love for social media, I transformed my career trajectory. I used these digital tools to build my marketing and communications business from the ground up, aiding clients in enhancing their brand strategies, marketing campaigns, and social media management. As I delved deeper, I learned all the tricks of the trade and helped my clients revamp their engagement and content, but I didn't stop there.

Just as the landscape of social media evolved, so did I. I eagerly embraced every upgrade, decoded every algorithm change, and explored every new platform. My curiosity led me to uncharted territories, and I found myself drawn into the fascinating worlds of podcasting, Web3, and NFTs.

In these new ventures, I discovered a refreshing resurgence of that precious commodity—community. The camaraderie I found in podcasting circles, NFT groups, and Facebook groups far exceeded what current social media platforms offered. I saw a return to social media's original intent: to connect, to be social.

In the face of these exciting developments, I was inspired to create this book. My mission is to share the story of social media's evolution, its roots, its journey, and its future direction. I want to help readers, followers, and clients reinvigorate their social media accounts with a genuine sense of community. I aim to empower you to create meaningful connections and build relationships rooted in the know-like-trust factor.

If you've ever felt frustrated or struggled to build connections or community on social media, this book is for you. It's a journey back to social media's original intent, peppered with insight and encouragement on how to take control of your accounts and reconfigure them for the future.

In the pages that follow, I offer explanations and stories sprinkled with motivation. By the end, I hope you'll not only understand the world of social media and the upcoming shift to Web3, but also feel equipped to harness these platforms' potential to create communities that people truly want to be a part of. I hope this book serves as an inspiring and helpful guide for your journey.

Introduction

Pssst—yes you! Do you secretly feel social media is a necessary evil for your business? Or maybe you obsessively stay up late at night trying to embrace every new platform, struggling to figure out features and how you can master them to stand out above the competition. You know it's the next big thing but struggle to keep up or feel overwhelmed. At some point, you cross your fingers and hope the next new platform or trend is just a blip—a fad—so you wave it off and tell yourself you don't need it.

If this sounds familiar, you are not alone. The speed and saturation of social media are beyond extraordinary when looking at the data. Our World in Data reports:

- Social media use among US adults increased from 5 percent in 2005 to 79 percent in 2019.

- Social media is now incorporated into the everyday life of one-third of the world's population.

Of course, this isn't new information, but the stats are eye-opening. Even more astonishing is how social media influences and modifies our behavior. We make purchasing decisions based on Facebook ads and carefully crafted algorithms. I mean, look at how it's changed your behavior—staying up all hours of the night to see what is trending or working to find the next thing, whatever that is now.

So yes, feeling it is a necessary evil isn't so far off. Keeping up with what's popular is important, especially when we know trends, and social connections can enhance engagement with us and our business. The problem is, we have lost perspective. When we think of social media, we think of likes, shares, going viral, misinformation, ad campaigns, and photo filters. What gets lost in the noise is the fundamentals of community and connection.

The power of community on social media is not something to be underestimated. It's the lifeblood of these platforms, the driving force behind their relevance and growth. Above all, it provides a sense of belonging and connection, something so critical in today's increasingly isolated world.

One example that instantly comes to mind is a client of mine, a small-business owner who had been struggling with building an online presence. Despite the client's best efforts, his posts seemed to vanish into the vast void of the internet, barely reaching a handful of people, let alone resonating with them.

When we began working together, one of the first things we did was shift the focus toward community building. Instead of creating posts in isolation, we started fostering conversations, sparking discussions, and actively engaging with the followers. We made a concerted effort to interact with other like-minded businesses, lending our support and sharing their content where relevant.

Slowly but surely, we began to see a change. The followers, once passive observers, were now actively involved, commenting, sharing, and even advocating for the brand. This sense of community breathed new life into the brand's online presence. It was no longer just a business—it had become a valued member of a broader online community.

This personal experience reaffirmed my belief in the power of community on social media. It's a beacon for those seeking connection, a space where like-minded individuals can come together, share their interests and values, and find a sense of belonging. Building a community on social media is not just about increasing your follower count; it's about creating meaningful, lasting relationships.

This sense of connection fostered through online communities can indeed wield considerable power in enhancing our emotional resilience and well-being. Contrary to popular belief that social media may harm mental health, it's important to note the potential it holds for positive impact when used appropriately. A study published in the Journal of Medical Internet Research emphasizes this point.

The study found that people who actively engaged in online communities, particularly ones centered on shared interests or challenges, reported lower levels of stress and improved overall well-being. These individuals felt more understood and less alone in their experiences, which contributed to their psychological resilience.

However, it's important to note that these benefits hinge on the quality of the interactions rather than the quantity. Passive scrolling, comparison culture, and negative interactions can indeed negatively impact mental health. It's when we shift from being passive consumers to active participants, engaging in meaningful conversations and nurturing positive relationships, that we can experience these psychological benefits.

In essence, it's not the platform itself that determines its impact on our mental health, but how we choose to use it. Harnessing the power of community and positive engagement on social media can lead to improved well-being, underlining the importance of conscious and purposeful social media usage.

An indispensable aspect of community on social media lies in its potential for knowledge exchange and collaboration. By actively participating in these virtual communities, we expose ourselves to a broad spectrum of ideas, experiences, and perspectives, setting the stage for both personal and professional growth.

Let me illustrate this with an example from my own journey. When I first ventured into the realm of Web3, I was a novice, intrigued but unsure where to begin. It was through my active participation in NFT-focused X communities and Discord groups that I started to grasp the nuances of this fascinating space. I was able to engage in meaningful discussions, learn from seasoned experts, and even share my own burgeoning insights.

But the benefits extended beyond mere learning. Through these communities, I found collaborators for my NFT Ninja Podcast, guests who brought along a wealth of knowledge and enriching perspectives. We worked together on several initiatives, collectively striving to demystify the world of NFTs for our audience.

This firsthand experience was incredibly enriching for me, both personally and professionally. I not only expanded my knowledge but also formed partnerships and collaborations that would have been unimaginable otherwise. This instance reiterates that social media communities are not just platforms for idle chatter; they can be vibrant hubs of collaborative learning and growth, providing immense value when navigated strategically.

A couple years ago, our agency had the chance to be part of an impactful grassroots movement that showed the power of community on social media. We began working with a local community leader, Karen, who was seeking to unseat a long-term incumbent on the town council. This official had been in place nearly two decades without serious contest.

Karen had passion and vision, but not much name recognition in the broader community. We helped her leverage social media to directly engage with voters. She shared her values, background, and goals for the town. But more importantly, she listened to the concerns voiced by residents in the comments and at neighborhood meetings.

Her followers began sharing Karen's posts and connecting her with other local influencers. Momentum built as she established herself as a viable alternative by authentically interacting with people. Volunteers from the community offered to aid her campaign. Donations rolled in from online supporters.

In the end, Karen won the election in a historic upset, defeating the incumbent by just a few hundred votes. The town council now better reflects the community it serves. This experience demonstrated that social media can rapidly amplify voices and movements previously shut out. By uniting a community behind a common cause, real change is possible. I'm proud our agency could play a small role in this grassroots victory

Overall, the importance of community on social media cannot be understated. It provides a sense of belonging, connection, and purpose that is essential to our well-being and happiness. By actively participating in online communities and building relationships with others, we can create a more positive, connected, and meaningful experience on social media.

As we've seen through personal examples and practical applications, social media, when used strategically, can foster connection, enable knowledge exchange, and even drive social change. Bringing all these elements together in a corporate context, we find compelling examples of businesses leveraging social media communities to amplify their values and mission.

One such business that embodies this comprehensive approach is Patagonia, the renowned outdoor clothing company. From its inception, Patagonia has built its brand around staunch commitments to environmental sustainability and social responsibility. This ethos is palpable not only in its eco-conscious products and business practices but also in its thoughtful use of social media.

Patagonia's social media channels serve as more than mere marketing platforms for the company's products; they are dynamic spaces where the company's core values come alive. Content centered on environmental issues, outdoor adventure stories, and conservation initiatives are routine, aligning with and reinforcing the brand's mission.

The company doesn't just broadcast, but it also actively listens and engages with its followers.

Patagonia has hosted live Q&A sessions on Instagram, featuring company executives and environmental activists, to foster open dialogue about sustainability and outdoor ethics. These interactive sessions have given followers a chance to have their concerns addressed directly, making them feel more personally connected to the brand.

Moreover, Patagonia's Worn Wear program is another fantastic demonstration of community building and value alignment. This initiative, frequently highlighted on its social media, encourages customers to send in their worn-out Patagonia clothing for repair, resale, or recycling—an effort to prolong product life-span and reduce environmental impact. Not only does this underline Patagonia's commitment to sustainability, but it also emphasizes the brand's focus on long-term customer value over immediate sales.

Another standout initiative is the Patagonia Action Works program, an activist network that uses social media to connect concerned individuals with environmental NGOs. Through Action Works posts, followers can find opportunities for volunteering, petition signing, and even direct donating. By extending its role from an outdoor gear provider to a facilitator of social action, Patagonia has turned its social media platform into a hub of environmental activism.

Through such transparent, authentic, and values-aligned actions, Patagonia has fostered a strong, loyal community on social media. This online community—customers, fans, and environmental enthusiasts who resonate deeply with the brand's mission—has significantly contributed to Patagonia's success. Its sustained engagement has helped bolster Patagonia's reputation as not just a leader in the outdoor industry, but a pioneering force in corporate social responsibility.

It's not just large brands that have focused on community-first with their social media efforts. During the pandemic, many small businesses, including coffee shops, struggled to stay afloat as the economy took a downturn and people were forced to stay at home. The story of Kyle, the owner of the Denver-based coffee shop (Torpedo Coffee), is a case in point for using social media in difficult times. Kyle was able to stay in business by embracing social media and joining local Facebook groups to connect with his community.

Kyle knew that the traditional way of doing business would not work during the pandemic, and he needed to come up with a new strategy. So he turned to social media and joined several Facebook groups that were based in his local community. In these groups, he introduced himself and his coffee shop, and he began to engage with the members by asking them what types of food and drinks they would like to see, and what hours they would be able to visit his shop if it were open.

Kyle was able to collect valuable feedback from the community members, and he used this information to adapt his business to meet their needs. He managed to source different types of coffee and food items that the community requested, and he also set up a schedule that worked for the majority of members who were available to visit the shop.

To make it more convenient for people, he also started a preorder system that allows customers to place their orders online and choose their pickup time, so that their drink would be ready when they arrive.

As a result of his efforts, Kyle was able to open his coffee shop a few days a week, and he had a steady stream of customers coming through the door. Many of them were members of the Facebook groups where he had connected with them, and they were excited to finally be able to try the shop's food and drinks.

Thanks to Kyle's innovative thinking and willingness to adapt, his coffee shop was able to survive during the pandemic, and he even managed to build a stronger relationship with his community. His efforts have shown the importance of connection, communication, and adaptability during hard times to remain in business.

The pandemic forced all of us to shift. Many brick-and-mortar businesses that had never given social media a second thought soon realized this was now their main priority. And not just for making sales but for connecting. Even as users, social media played a crucial role in helping us to maintain connections and build community. As the world went into lockdown and we were unable to physically be with one another, social media provided a way for us to stay connected and support one another through difficult times.

However, now that the pandemic is in the rearview mirror, it seems that many have forgotten the importance of social media for building connections and community. With the return to more normal circumstances, people may be more inclined to rely on in-person interactions and neglect the online communities that they cultivated during the pandemic.

It's disappointing that people seem to have lost that sense of community and connection we found on social media during the pandemic. But it's important to remember that social media isn't just for entertainment or self-promotion; it can be a powerful tool for building real connections and supporting each other, especially during tough times.

That's why we need to keep using social media in a way that brings us together. Whether it's joining online groups, commenting on and sharing other people's posts, or just sending a message to a friend, there are plenty of ways to keep the connections we made strong. It's up to us to keep these connections alive and keep building community on social media.

Back to Basics

From the groundbreaking telegraph to today's social media giant, Meta (formerly Facebook), these platforms were, and still are, tools designed to foster human connections. They enable communication; the sharing of information, personal stories, photos, and videos; and build communities. Any subsequent uses or implications are, in essence, by-products or unintended consequences of their primary purpose.

It all started with the first ". . . - - - . . ." transmitted through a telegraph. If you're not familiar with Morse Code, this sequence stands for SOS, a universal distress signal used in emergencies. From there, we evolved to pagers, where number sequences became coded messages. "07734," for instance, may look like a random number, but when viewed upside down, it cleverly spells "hello." Fast-forward to the present, and we find a whole new language in text messaging, where a simple "☺" conveys warmth and happiness.

However, somewhere along the line, social media morphed from a communication tool into a marketing vehicle. As marketers, we must admit, we have a propensity for adapting platforms to our advantage. But in this sea of consumerism, it's crucial that we remember and refocus on the fundamentals—community and connection. Prioritize these aspects, and everything else will naturally align.

No matter where the future of social media takes us, you'll be equipped to adapt and excel. I assure you of that!

Observing the trends, it's clear to see that the social media evolution shows no signs of halting. Some of the most influential tech companies worldwide are continually pouring resources into developing cutting-edge features poised to redefine social media as we know it.

The tempo of technological advancements is accelerating, with social media platforms persistently exploring novel and exciting ways to captivate their users and elevate the overall experience.

In this dynamic era, where change is the only constant, it's evident that the journey of social media is far from its final destination. These continuous investments and rapid innovations by the tech giants highlight the unequivocal fact—that social media isn't just sticking around; it's surging forward and reshaping itself, and the world around it, in real time.

Indeed, a shining example of this relentless innovation in social media can be seen through the incorporation of artificial intelligence (AI) and machine learning. These technologies are rapidly transforming the landscape, personalizing the user experience, and making content more relevant to each unique user.

To put this into context, let's consider a platform like Spotify. By analyzing data generated by user interactions—the songs you play, skip, or add to your playlist—Spotify's AI-driven algorithms can curate a personalized Discover Weekly playlist. This feature presents you with a weekly collection of songs aligning with your musical tastes, introducing you to new artists and tracks that you're likely to enjoy. The algorithm essentially learns your preferences over time, further refining your personalized content with each interaction.

Similarly, consider Netflix. It uses AI to enhance its recommendation system. Based on your viewing history, genres you frequently watch, and even how you rate shows, Netflix suggests movies and TV shows that you might like. The algorithm gets more accurate the more you interact with the platform, consistently enhancing your user experience.

These examples underscore how AI and machine learning are revolutionizing social media platforms, providing individual users with an experience uniquely tailored to their preferences. This trend is likely to continue, with AI's role in shaping the user experience set to become even more integral in the future.

Let's dive deeper into this by looking at a few distinct examples of social media platforms that have been created with niche communities in mind.

Take Behance, for instance, a platform specifically designed for creatives such as artists, designers, and photographers. It allows users to showcase their work, gain inspiration from others, and network with potential clients or collaborators. Users can comment on one another's work, participate in creative challenges, and even find job opportunities, effectively fostering a specialized community that supports and encourages creative growth.

Likewise, Twitch is a prime example of a social media platform tailored to a particular niche—gamers. On Twitch, gamers can live-stream their gameplay, chat with viewers in real time, and even monetize their streams through donations, subscriptions, and ads. Twitch is more than just a platform for sharing gaming content; it's a hub for fostering a passionate community of like-minded individuals who can connect, collaborate, and share their love for gaming.

In terms of more interactive and immersive experiences, platforms like Facebook have delved into virtual reality through products like Oculus. Users can put on a VR headset and suddenly find themselves in virtual chat rooms or gaming environments with friends, offering a new dimension to social connection and community building.

Another instance of this trend toward immersive experiences is the popularity of Instagram's live-streaming feature, which allows users to host real-time video streams. Followers can tune in, drop comments, and engage directly with the host, creating a more immediate and interactive social media experience.

These platforms and technological developments illustrate the continued push toward more niche, interactive, and immersive social media experiences. This trend continues to open new doors for social connection and community building, redefining how we perceive and engage with social media.

Indeed, the line between social media and e-commerce has become increasingly blurred as many platforms incorporate direct purchasing capabilities. This trend is known as "social commerce," and it offers users the convenience of seamless shopping experiences right within the confines of their favorite social platforms. Rather than redirecting users to an external website to make a purchase, users can now view and buy products without leaving their news feeds, effectively transforming social browsing into social shopping.

To illustrate this, let's consider a personal experience involving Billie, a direct-to-consumer razor company. One day, as I was scrolling through my Instagram feed, I came across a beautifully designed post by Billie. It was an eye-catching video showcasing the company's latest razor model, with a bold claim about its superior performance and convenience.

Intrigued, I clicked on the Shop Now button integrated into the post. Within seconds, a product page popped up within Instagram itself, detailing the razor's features, reviews, and price. The whole transaction, from selecting the color of the razor to making the payment, took place in a swift, smooth process within Instagram. No website redirections, no interruptions—just a streamlined, user-friendly shopping experience that blended social media browsing with e-commerce.

The integration of social media and e-commerce is more than just a novel feature—it's a strategic move that taps into the potential of impulse buying, leverages the power of social proof, and enriches user engagement with brands. As seen from the Billie example, this strategy could potentially reshape how we perceive and interact with social media and e-commerce in the future.

The next significant frontier of social media evolution, attracting significant investments from big tech companies, are the concepts of Web3 and non-fungible tokens (NFTs). Web3 denotes the next iteration of the internet, underpinned by blockchain technology. This empowers users with enhanced control over their data and facilitates decentralized, peer-to-peer transactions, marking a decisive shift from the traditional centralized internet model.

NFTs are a unique form of digital assets, each distinct and irreplaceable, essentially acting as a digital certificate of ownership. These tokens can represent a myriad of digital items, including art, virtual real estate, or even digital collectibles. Their uniqueness and tradability on decentralized marketplaces give them unprecedented value in the digital realm.

Not merely treating them as a topic of research, big tech companies are actively investing in the potential of Web3 and NFTs to radically transform our digital interactions and the way content is monetized. Consider a scenario where a social media platform utilizes NFTs to create a dynamic marketplace, allowing users to buy and sell unique digital assets like photos, videos, or 3D models. These assets, apart from their original value, could be shared, remixed, and reinvented by others, further driving their desirability and utility.

Web3 and NFTs are also being leveraged to create more immersive, interactive social experiences. Users can own and personalize virtual items and spaces, interacting with them in real time, fostering a sense of digital ownership and community. The video game Decentraland, for example, allows users to purchase and personalize virtual land with NFTs, creating an immersive social experience.

While still in its infancy, the integration of Web3 and NFTs into the fabric of social media is an arena of active research, development, and significant investment from big tech companies. A prime example is Facebook's recent rebranding as "Meta Platforms Inc.," or simply "Meta," to underscore its commitment to building the "metaverse," a shared, immersive, and interactive virtual space that expands on the principles of Web3.

Such advancements have immense potential to redefine our engagement with digital content, the ways we create and monetize it, and even how we collaborate on various projects. In this context, the inclusion of NFTs can foster a unique sense of digital ownership, leading to new avenues for content creation and monetization.

Moreover, Web3 enhances the capacity for decentralized interaction and collaboration, potentially bringing a paradigm shift in how we connect with others online. The exploration of Web3 and NFTs, as evidenced by Meta's bold strides into the metaverse, heralds a promising era for the evolution of social media. The journey has just begun, and its potential ramifications are exciting and far-reaching.

The implementation of Web3 and NFTs in social media is still in its early stages, but it's an area of research and development that many big tech companies are investing in. These advancements have the potential to change how we interact with digital content, how we create and monetize it, and how we connect with others in different projects, and that's why it's considered a promising area for social media evolution.

Overall, it is clear that the evolution of social media is ongoing, and that big tech companies are investing significant resources in the development of new features and technologies that will shape the future of social media. While it is impossible to predict exactly what the future holds, one thing is certain: Social media will continue to play a major role in how we connect, communicate, and engage with one another.

I have been dialing in and following social media and broadcasting trends for as long as I can remember. As a child, I always had a passion for radio. While other girls were playing with Barbies and baby dolls, I spent hours recording radio shows on cassette tapes in my room. I had the luxury of growing up alongside the internet and social media.

While I was working at the college radio station, one of my jobs was to get bands and record labels to send us their music to play for—gasp—free. While many of my counterparts were sending handwritten letters in the mail, I decided to venture into this new social media website called MySpace. Soon the station was receiving music by the boxful. In addition to receiving all this new music, I was creating relationships with many up-and-coming bands. I quickly discovered how incredible the tool MySpace could be and how fast relationships could be made online. After graduating, I was fortunate enough to land my dream job as a sports broadcaster for the Colorado Rockies, Denver Broncos, Colorado Avalanche, and Denver Nuggets.

Then I got hit with the next thing—the invention of SiriusXM radio.

In my world, SiriusXM felt like a death sentence—the end of radio. Everyone in the industry freaked out. I thought I needed to shift with the tide before everyone else jumped ship. As a marketing manager, I was writing scripts, placing media buys, and running marketing campaigns, and I could still dip my toe into the social media world that I had become entranced with in college.

In doing so, I embraced the notion that social media isn't about selling, posting, and talking at people—it is about building a sense of community, engaging at a human level, and sharing a richer experience. Back in the early 2000s, we didn't have phones that could instantly upload 4K video. It was a community-first, a conversation-first, way of connecting. It wasn't just about selling, promoting, likes, or followers. It was about building a sense of community and engagement. It was about fostering a connection with your audience and creating a shared experience that was meaningful and fulfilling. By embracing this from an early stage, I was able to quickly make connections with people I probably never would have met otherwise.

Eventually, I heard about podcasting, but like many, I first examined the trend from a distance. I was curious because it spoke to my inner radio host. But I had no idea what to say or how to even get started. Like many during April 2020, I was given the gift of time; what better time than now, so why not give it a try? So I purchased my first microphone, and the Rocky Mountain Marketing Podcast was born. I quickly learned that the only differences between radio and podcasting were the mode of transportation (radio waves versus RSS feeds) and the flexibility or opportunity within the community. For all the fear I initially had, in the end, it was like second nature. And as they say—the rest is history. Well, sort of . . .

Now my curiosity and passion for community building have segued into NFTs, creator coins, and the wonderful world of Web3. Don't worry—I'll get to that later, but it isn't as complicated and scary as it sounds!

The Future

I see a vision of the future and how the original intent of social media is coming back around. The purpose of this book is to bring light to the history and evolution of social media, which will help us see where it's going and how you can maximize your TIME on social media to grow an engaged community. By doing so, we can reconnect with the basics, plan for the future, and help you build your business using social media as that tool. Social media and social media marketing should be about bringing value, solving a problem, or creating an authentic and genuine experience for your audience.

Social media was designed as a means to communicate with one another. Sadly, we have evolved to consume—scroll, swipe, click. So many social media strategies fail because we focus on selling, going viral, or gaining followers and not on connecting or creating community. But that is all changing! The metaverse and Web3 are about offering a more immersive experience, dialing in on this need for a sense of belonging, no matter where you call home.

Now social media is a window to let people get to know you. People want to do business with people they know, like, and trust. There is a movement to buy local and support small business and keep local economies going. If people know you, like you, and trust you, they are more likely to buy your product or service and often are even willing to pay more than they would if they went to a big-box store. Social media allows us to share our authentic self with the community. The more personal experience is what the consumer craves, and the future of social media, Web3 and the metaverse is what will help build a rich experience that is more engaging.

If you're sitting there thinking, "I have no idea what the metaverse or Web3 is," don't fret. This book will deliver a comprehensive and digestible rundown on these concepts. You'll journey through the social media timeline, technologies, terminology, and strategies from their nascent stages to their current form. You will delve into the world of NFTs—not as an investment, but as an opportunity for building community and significantly enhancing your social media presence.

The first half of this book is your time machine, transporting you through the history of social media, illuminating how each technology or platform transitioned from communication and community focus to a consumerism-oriented model optimized for profits. The second half is your road map, guiding you on how to leverage social media, not solely for profit, but more importantly, to cultivate an authentic, community-driven experience for your followers. And in doing so, you'll be ready to ride the wave of whatever comes next in this ever-evolving digital landscape.

Are you ready?!

———

Chapter 1

Original Intent of Social Media

Ahhh . . . the early days of social media. Are you old enough to remember?

When we think of social media now, there are a lot of mixed opinions. One view is that social media is a necessity. We need it as a way to advertise business, find recommendations for the local plumber or painter, and keep up to date with local news and events. Another view is that social media is divisive, spreading misinformation while monetizing personal data, and needs to be regulated. While it is true that social media has had unintended consequences, the original intent was not what we see now.

The original basic concept for what we now know as social media was to create an alternative medium for communication. Simply, social media took the written word and transformed messages into electronic communication traveling faster than snail mail by way of the phone line. Of course, balking at the idea, nonbelievers would ask why you couldn't just pick up the telephone. Why do you need to write people a message they will need to read when you can call?! Ha!

In the beginning, the idea was a novelty. However, it didn't take long for email, bulletin boards, and chat rooms to catch on. Eventually, online spaces like AOL became THE PLACE to be. It was a place where people could connect with others, from anywhere, who shared similar interests. Early days consisted of tinkering with email and learning to attach and send photos to distant friends and family members. This new world would be a place for open dialogue and sharing of ideas. Social media platforms then became a forum for discussion and interaction, providing almost instant gratification. If you are old enough, you may remember the joy you felt hearing the infamous message "You've got mail." It was like opening a gift on your birthday.

Unfortunately, that is not what we see today. Somehow we now often feel burdened by social media. Scrolling through email and social feeds happens in the same way we walk to the pantry and grab the bag of chips—aimless eating even though we are not hungry. Yet we continue munching until we realize the chips are gone, and we are still unfulfilled. So what has changed?

Social media has changed a lot over the years; it's not just about connecting with friends and family anymore. Businesses feel the pressure to use it to sell their stuff, and that means we're swamped with ads, notifications, and other marketing messages. It can be overwhelming to sift through all that noise to find something interesting.

As business owners or entrepreneurs, we can fall into the trap of thinking we need to be talking AT people instead of connecting with them. We're focused on promoting our products and services and posting as much content as possible, just to see what sticks. But we often forget that social media is not just about selling; it's also about building a community, engaging with people, and sharing experiences.

We also forget that social media is not just about us sending out messages. It's about listening and engaging with our audience. It's about understanding what people want, what they need, and what they're interested in. And addressing those things in a way that is meaningful and relevant to them.

It's not only about getting new customers; social media also helps in keeping the existing ones. By engaging them with special offers, discounts, and promotions, and also being there for them when they need customer service or after-sales support, businesses can turn their customers into loyal ones and get positive word of mouth.

To sum it up, instead of just trying to sell and promote, businesses should focus on building community and truly engaging with their audience. By creating quality content and addressing their audience's needs, they'll create loyal customers and a successful business. So let's stop the constant promotion and start building connections instead.

The Nature of the Beast

This move from community to consumerism didn't happen overnight. It has taken decades and is the nature of our culture. I'm not just talking about social media either; we are a consumption-first society throughout every aspect of our lives. Our entire economy is based on consumption. If you don't believe me or perhaps do but are unsure how it came to be, let's take a little trip down memory lane.

Before the industrial revolution, most goods were produced and purchased through what is known as the "cottage industry," where goods were made in small batches from local homes or by the tradespeople of a community—funny enough, this is on the rise again. Eventually, factories and railroads allowed for the mass production and shipping of goods at greater distances in shorter time frames. At the same time, we began to see a rise in what we know as the middle class. This new class in society brought with it the desire to attain what it didn't have. By the Roaring Twenties, consumption and consumerism were on full display and commonplace. Unfortunately, it was short-lived with the stock market crash, the Great Depression, and the onset of World War II.

During the war, the sacrifice of goods manufacturing became

necessary, and people did their patriotic duty. Eventually, wartime production lifted the United States out of the Depression, and once the war was over, wages were higher, and Americans were ready to spend again. Historian Lizabeth Cohen explained that it was patriotic to be a consumer after the war because economic recovery depended on a "mass consumption economy." Americans eagerly answered the call to be VERY patriotic and went on spending sprees for cars, houses, modern appliances, and the newest kitchen gadgets.

By the fifties and sixties, goods became less expensive, and formal marketing campaigns based on psychology exploded. For example, many companies played on how a product fits into a person's sense of identity. A campaign would associate people's "social standing in society with their level and quality of consumption." This method is still used in advertising today. If you don't believe me and have teenagers around, just ask them. I assure you, at some point, you have heard, or they have said, "But Mo-ommmm, everyone is doing it" or "But Mo-ommmm, everyone has one"—not there yet? Throw a stone, and you will find them!

Unpacking the Purpose

This brief history lesson helps bring some clarity and understanding to how social media moved from a mode of communication to consumerism and how the original intent of social media became skewed. We went from connecting to interacting to advertising. In so many ways, we have been indoctrinated to shift everything to a consumption mindset. It's in our DNA—great capitalism at work.

Once you understand and see how the dots connect, it makes more sense. You can see how we are so engaged in social media from an aspect of selling, and we are saturated with advertising. It's like peeking behind the curtain at the great Wizard of Oz. You can see who is flipping switches and pulling levers. So remove the mystery, and you can better plan a course of action for the future. You can better position yourself to leverage social media in a way that most other businesses aren't—by getting back to the basics.

When I suggest we "get back to basics," I'm not proposing that we abandon social media altogether and revert to pre-digital methods of communication like letters, phone calls, or even faxes. While these traditional means—letters, phone calls, and faxes—are still utilized today, their role has been significantly transformed. Take the real estate industry as a perfect example. In the past, real estate and mortgage brokers would distribute calendars, sports schedules, and recipe calendars through regular mail. Then email emerged on the scene. It was seen as a novelty, and early adopters, in a bid to showcase their tech savviness, were quick to embrace it.

We got so caught up in the instant gratification and low cost of email that we've lost touch with traditional means of communication, like writing in cursive or addressing an envelope. Why spend time writing a letter and sending it through mail when it's faster and more convenient to type out a message and send it through the internet? But now we have started to see a shift.

Nowadays, people are looking for more meaningful connections and authentic interactions; they crave the personal touch that digital communication lacks. Studies have shown that people are more likely to remember and respond to a physical message than an email or text. With the increasing amount of digital clutter, physical mail can stand out and be more effective.

Moreover, people also realize that the internet is not a secure space and the convenience of digital communication has its own cost, the loss of privacy. People are now taking a step back to secure their information and going back to traditional ways of communication.

Another aspect is that as the world becomes more digitized, it has also become more impersonal. People want to feel a connection with the person or business they are interacting with, something that digital communication can't always provide. Businesses are now starting to realize this, and they are going back to more personal communication methods like direct mail campaigns and personalized phone calls.

Now getting back to basics doesn't mean going back to pre-digital times, but rather finding a balance between digital and traditional communication methods. By embracing the benefits of both, we can create meaningful connections, secure our information, and stand out in the digital world. It's about finding a balance and leveraging the strengths of both to create an optimal and effective communication strategy.

Coming Full Circle

Now we are bombarded with email, and inboxes everywhere are saturated. The laborious task of skimming and deleting every day leads to irritation and automatically clicking Spam and Unsubscribe buttons. Over the last decade, much has been written and reported on how email has lost its punch. The novelty has worn off, and email has become impersonal.

So as with real estate brokers, many of us have swung back to hand-written letters, birthday cards, and thank you notes. After all, the only things showing up in the mailbox these days are credit card offers and political ads, right?! Old-fashioned mail is back, and it feels like Christmas every time we get an unexpected and personal note!

But why does the hand-written letter or thank you note still work? Why have many businesses gone back to it? Because it is personal—it shows that a little effort and care went into the process. When you send an individual note or card, you speak directly to the person it is addressed to. It takes longer to write a message, stuff an envelope, address it, and walk it to the mailbox. There is no spam or mass mailing of original hand-written messages. It is unique, engaging, and THOUGHTFUL.

Now take that process and apply it to social media. Social media was meant to communicate, engage, share information, and, eventually, work as a way to connect people across distances that have similar interests. Yet it has become an impersonal violation of our digital space. In many ways, social media posts and ads are the latest version of door-to-door sales at dinner time, spam text messages during a massage, or ding-dong ditchers at one in the morning. Gone are the days of the Facebook wall. (Remember that?) Let's take a quick trip down memory lane . . .

Once upon a time, Facebook was a simpler place. When you logged in, you were greeted with a wall, a blank space where you could post updates, photos, and links for all your friends to see. It was a virtual bulletin board where you could keep tabs on what your friends were up to and share your own experiences with them.

For many people, the Facebook wall was a way of staying connected with friends and family, even if they were physically far away. People would take the time to craft thoughtful messages, post photos from their daily lives, and comment on one another's updates. It was a way of building a sense of community, of sharing a piece of your life with others and feeling like you were a part of something bigger.

In September 2006, Facebook unleashed a seismic change that would forever alter the platform. They introduced the news feed, replacing the chronological profile walls that had defined the Facebook experience.

Mark Zuckerberg unveiled this new personalized, algorithmic feed late one evening. Zuckerberg introduced the news feed in a controversial blog post presenting it as a discovery tool to help you "keep up with what your friends are doing." But for many loyal users, this removal of control fractured their tight-knit communities.

The news feed used engagement data to curate a constantly updated stream of content tailored to each user's interests and behaviors. Gone were the communal walls where you choose what to share. Now an AI decided which posts were shown based on popularity and comments. Friends' updates were buried if not sufficiently "newsworthy."

Long-winded complaints and eulogies for the walls quickly flooded the site. Over 17,000 users joined a "Facebook News Feed Protest" group. Critiques centered around lack of control and privacy. The feed felt impersonal and shattered their online communities. But Zuckerberg dismissed concerns, insisting users just needed time to adjust.

This shift also cracked open the floodgates for advertising. With content sorted by engagement signals, brands could now micro target users based on interests and behaviors. Facebook ads instantly became more effective and valuable.

At first ads were humble text units easily overlooked. But soon video ads, full screen takeovers, and "sponsored content" came to dominate. By 2009, Facebook's ads increased 90% year-over-year. Users struggled to find posts from actual friends amongst the onslaught.

Initially ads appeared sparingly and discreetly. But within a few years, video ads auto-playing with sound, splashy full screen takeovers, and "sponsored content" disguised as regular posts came to dominate. Users were overwhelmed trying to spot posts from friends among the barrage.

The communal, connection-driven Facebook had eroded. In its place was a noisy marketplace driven by clicks and conversions. The change was pivotal, marking the definitive shift of social media towards consumerism.

While controversial, the news feed formula proved incredibly lucrative. Facebook's advertising model resulted in exponential revenue growth. But it came at the cost of the user experience, leaving many nostalgic for the simple days of walls and real connections.

For many users, the addition of ads in their news feed made the platform feel less like a place to connect with friends and family and more like a place to be sold to. This change made the social media experience less enjoyable, as ads and notifications started to overpower posts from friends and family. Users also found it difficult to see the posts from friends and family, as the news feed algorithm prioritized the posts that Facebook deemed most relevant or profitable to itself.

In short, the launch of the news feed changed the way people used Facebook, and many users felt that it led to a loss of community and the personal touch that they had come to enjoy, which was now replaced by the commercialism.

As Facebook evolved, businesses recognized the immense marketing potential of its platform and reach. Highly targeted ads enabled by users' data transformed organic content into paid messages.

Facebook launched demographic targeting in 2007, letting brands serve ads by age, location, interests and more. Hyper-specific behavioral targeting followed, using activity like page visits to determine recipients. Suddenly ads could incorporate users' declared and undeclared data to feel personalized, not promotional.

The onslaught was relentless. By 2012, sponsored posts accounted for 25% of feeds. Pages that users followed were buried under ads. Facebook ads had increased over 400% between 2009-2012. Critics raised privacy concerns around the granular data targeting enabled this. But revenues skyrocketed in parallel.

The communal network where users freely interacted was now an e-commerce site. Brands could pay to insert themselves into the community. User experience suffered as ads and algorithms took priority over friends.

Many yearned for the intimacy of Facebook's early days as a digital extension of social life. Now commercial interests had marginalized users in favor of profits and growth. Finding balance seemed impossible amidst the gold rush.

Leadership dismissed criticisms and ignored the loss of community in pursuit of engagement and revenues. They repeatedly claimed changes improved relevance and empowered businesses. But many wondered what was lost for the sake of money and metrics.

The challenge remains to ensure that social media platforms can serve as both vibrant marketplaces and spaces for genuine social interaction. This is a delicate act of balancing, and the future of social media may well depend on how successfully this equilibrium is achieved.

But as social media continues to evolve and businesses adapt to these changes, it's crucial to keep the fundamentals at the heart of your approach—fostering both a sense of community and authentic engagement. Achieving success on social media isn't solely about the frequency of your posts or the amount of time and money you invest, but rather about comprehending the medium and the historical context of consumerism and applying this knowledge creatively and strategically.

Drawing an analogy with art, consider different artists. One artist might excel in oil painting, adept at complex blending techniques and the creation of exquisite gradations of color. Another might be a skilled sculptor, capable of transforming a block of stone or a lump of clay into a tangible, three-dimensional masterpiece. However, what unites them is their grounding in the fundamental concepts of their craft and an understanding of its history and evolution. They adapt their techniques to the characteristics of their chosen medium to create compelling pieces of art.

Applying this to social media, it's essential to understand the evolution of the medium. This knowledge enables you to better navigate its complexities, adapt to its ongoing changes, and harness the current trends to your advantage.

As we trace the evolution of social media through the decades, it's evident that the landscape has shifted significantly from the early communal days of connection and sharing. Today, the constant pressure to create content and stay active leads many business owners and marketers to social media fatigue.

But what if there was a better way to leverage these platforms without burning yourself out? A strategic approach to achieve real results while actually posting less? Later in the book, I'll reveal a proven four-post formula for doing just that—maximizing your social media impact while maintaining sanity. This step-by-step framework blends informative and helpful content with judicious promotion to organically convert and engage your audience.

By spacing out promotional posts with value-adding content, you can increase reach and conversions efficiently. I'll unpack the awareness-to-action model fully in upcoming chapters. But for now, know that more thoughtful posting can achieve greater success amid the social media frenzy. The four-post blueprint offers clarity in the ever-evolving digital landscape. And it aligns perfectly with social media's original purpose— fostering connections, not just spamming sales pitches.

To truly succeed on social media, businesses must shift their focus from promoting their products and services to building a sense of community and engaging with their audience. They must focus on creating high-quality, engaging content that will capture the attention of their target audience and foster a sense of connection and community. They must also be responsive to the needs and interests of their audience, and address them in a way that is meaningful and relevant.

Businesses today must realize that social media is not just a tool for marketing and advertising; it is a powerful tool for building connections and fostering community. Businesses that focus on building a sense of community and engaging with their audience will be able to create loyal customers and a thriving business. So instead of simply throwing content out there and hoping that your audience will come, it's important to think about how your content is building a community around your business.

So let's take a journey to explore the media used in social media!

Chapter 2

In the Beginning

When we think of the history and evolution of social media, most often we only go as far back as MySpace (now known as Myspace). However, social media has a longer history than you might expect. In reality, social media is older than the internet. Think about it—the fundamentals of social media are communication and connection. Thus we have to travel back in time and work our way forward. This overemphasis on promotion loses sight of the original community-building spirit of social media. My four-post strategy, unveiled later on, will show you how to recapture that balance.

Now you may argue that this is ridiculous and that social media couldn't exist before the internet. If so, I would ask you to think back to the original intent of social media. If it is a means of communicating and connecting people, what technology made that happen? When you think of social media in this respect, it becomes easier to follow the trail.

The Grandfather of Social Media

I know it sounds crazy, but hear me out. The telegraph was a revolutionary technological advance that started the information era in 1844. It allowed for faster communication and data transfer over long distances. The technology worked by sending electrical signals over a wire between two points.

Hmm—this transfer of data across a wire kind of sounds like the internet.

Now let's think about the language. The telegraph is a machine that uses Morse Code. Morse Code is a two-symbol system of dots and dashes in a series to communicate numbers and letters of the alphabet. Sound familiar? It should! Computers use programs, and these programs are built using what we call binary coding. Binary code is also a two-symbol system, similar to Morse Code, using 1s and 0s to create letters, numbers, words, characters, and instructions for computer games and applications.

Each technology uses a two-symbol system to transfer data between two locations or devices. However, Morse Code is the grandfather of binary coding. Telegraph technology not only is the grandfather of the internet and shaped the landscape of how information or data is transferred but is the basis for computer coding and IT infrastructure as a whole.

Of course, there were other methods of transferring data and information across distances long before the telegraph. For example, the semaphore was perhaps mother to the electric telegraph. The semaphore was a series of signal stations located on hilltops. The method of communication relied on massive movable arms that signaled numbers and letters. On one end, the message was laid out with the arms; at the other, the receiver would watch through a telescope and decipher the message.

The issue with the semaphore was its reliance on visibility—factors like weather often hindered its usefulness. For this reason, the semaphore, along with smoke signals, fire beacons, and drumbeats would not be considered the start of social media technology. The telegraph was a major advancement because it transmitted electrical signals through wires, eliminating the need for an unobstructed line of sight between sender and receiver. By using Morse Code, the telegraph allowed for long distance communication unaffected by weather or terrain, making it the first technology that could reliably send messages across great distances. This was a revolutionary development that paved the way for future social media and communication tools.

Following this train of thought, you may think other forms of communication or technology are more influential than the telegraph for creating social media as we know it today. I would argue that everything after the telegraph, while significant, is a mere cousin.

Social Media's Cousin

The telegraph, a monumental leap in technology that originated in the 1830s and took hold in 1844 with Morse sending the first coded message, spurred a series of further advancements. One such evolution is the invention of the radio—a subject I'm quite passionate about!

Though I am enthusiastic about discussing everything related to radio and audio, it's crucial to acknowledge that radio itself cannot be credited as the genesis of social media. The concept of radio blossomed in the 1890s, several decades after the advent of the telegraph. Historically, radio is often perceived as a wireless telegraph, given the similar thought processes behind the inventions.

However, radio's transformative power lies in its ability to foster communities and connectivity. Listeners across vast geographical expanses tuned in to their radios to hear music, news broadcasts, drama series, and more. The shared experience of listening, reacting, and discussing these programs created a sense of community and collective experience. In a way, this was an early, rudimentary form of social engagement that preceded digital social media platforms. The communal aspect of radio listening and the social interactions it encouraged were, in fact, a precursor to the dynamic online communities we see today.

You could argue that radio might be the offspring of the telegraph when looking at the intention of the inventor. While similar, they are different. The telegraph is limited to dots and dashes in coded messages. In contrast, the radio allows us to hear words being spoken. We no longer need to decode the message. Without the telegraph, it is possible that the vision for a wireless telegraph would never have come to be.

Radio broadcasting was the invention of an Italian, Guglielmo Marconi. His vision was to send a wireless telegraph, which he did in 1895 when he sent a Morse Code message to a designated point over a kilometer away. By 1897, his work earned him a patent for the radio. However, at the time, it was considered a wireless telegraph meant to send coded messages and not what we now know as radio.

It wasn't until the years leading up to World War I that scientists and inventors believed that radio had potential beyond dots and dashes. By 1914, radio was capable of transmitting voices and music across great distances. With the Roaring Twenties in full swing (no pun intended), radio boomed, and people found it the primary source of news and entertainment. Eighty percent of the US population owned a radio before 1940. However, there are always the naysayers.

Radio changed our behavior in ways we never imagined. In the 1920s, churches broadcast services, universities offered radio-based classes, and newspapers were "cross-posting" between print and radio broadcasts.

Impressive? Of course! Yet as impressive as it was, radio was still developed using the technology of the telegraph. The telegraph was the inspiration for all other technology due to both the transmission and coding.

Evolving Social Media Technology

Other sources of communicating and connecting people may not be as revolutionary as the telegraph or as sexy as the radio, but they are worth acknowledging. If nothing else, we need to recognize the evolving technologies for how they have influenced our behavior. From the telephone and two-way radios to the pager and eventually mobile phones, they all have a place in the social media conversation.

Let's start with the telephone. It's a wonderful communication device favored by teens through the ages, and keeping mothers frustrated for decades.

Tinkering with telephone technology started shortly after the invention of the telegraph. However, the first official telephone exchange didn't happen until 1877–1878. That flame sparked a fire, and by 1900, there were over a half a million phones in use. Five years later, there were over 2 million phones, and that number more than doubled by 1910.

The telephone proved indispensable for communication within a few short years. Proponents touted how the telephone would be a tool to allow mobility, make flexible work arrangements possible, aid emergency workers—and bring people closer together. It has done all those things, but it wasn't a straight line. As with any technology, it was clunky at first. There was a lot of user error, confusion, and even fear around the device.

In today's world, a mobile phone or application update can drive us mad due to the learning curve and changes made. In the early days of the telephone, problems were a little more rudimentary. Frustration was found in having to travel to the general store to make use of the contraption. Once phone lines entered the home, they were usually connected to what is known as a "party line," where multiple houses were tied to the same connection. Party lines were a source of entertainment and gossip, with switchboard operators and neighbors eavesdropping on conversations. With a party line, you had to wait for others to get off the phone so that you could use it.

Of course, the telephone evolved into the cordless phone and then into the mobile or cell phone. The device has changed drastically while the technology remains almost as it was (minus the party line).

The evolution of devices isn't limited to the phone. We can see how the technology of the telegraph morphed into radio and telephone. However, the same fundamentals apply to two-way radios, answering machines, voice mail, pagers, and even chatbots.

Think about the Morse Code for SOS—the dots and dashes. SOS is the universal symbol for distress or HELP even though it means "Save Our Ship." Now short sequences of letters have morphed and extended in even more creative ways. Back in the day when pagers were the hottest tech, you could send the message "Hello" by typing out 07734. Inverted the numbers become letters. "Hi" is 14, and inverted 371445 reads "Smile." Now we have LOL, OMG, and WTH intermixed with emojis.

That brings us closer to more familiar social media platforms and the early days of the internet.

Chapter 3

Social Media on a Trajectory

So often, the advancement of technology is spearheaded by the government. Social media isn't any different. After all, Morse Code, the radio, and the telephone were all supported and used by governments before and during conflicts. As it relates to digital communication, in 1969, the US Department of Defense created the Advanced Research Projects Agency Network (the ARPANET). Hmm—ARPANET—internet? This network allowed scientists at four interconnected universities to share data, programming, and hardware. In 1987, the National Science Foundation launched NSFNET, leading to the internet and social media platforms we became so familiar with by 1997.

The eighties and nineties launched services like CompuServe and America Online (AOL) with email, online chat rooms, and message boards. From there, the platform Six Degrees came online in 1997. It was a profile uploading service. By 1999, blogs gained traction, and the social gaming site called Friendster came online.

The early days of the internet and social media were all founded on what techies call Web 1.0.

Web 1.0

Web 1.0 is considered the first version of the internet and social web interactions. When we compare it with what we use now, it looks and sounds clunky and slow and not very exciting. However, at the time it was all the rage. If you know, you know! Who else remembers typing DOS commands into the computers or playing The Oregon Trail on the Apple computers at school.

If you were born after the early 2000s, Web 1.0 wasn't like what we experience today. First, you had to use the land telephone line to connect to the internet. You would disconnect the phone and plug in the computer. If you were playing a game on AOL and didn't have two phone lines, a phone call could interrupt your game. Once the computer was plugged in, the computer would dial a phone number and make terrible screeching sounds with some beeps and boops. When the screeching stopped, you could connect to the first internet browser, called the "WorldWideWeb"—as in the first three letters we know in a web address, "www," later named "Nexus."

Interacting with the WorldWideWeb was more like interacting with an online library. You would type in a web address and see a display of static pages with whatever information was published on that page. Experts in technology will tell you that Web 1.0 was a "read-only" web experience. There was no opportunity for interaction. For retail sites, you could browse products like a catalog but often had to email someone to place an order.

Then advertising on the Web 1.0 WorldWideWeb was banned! An internet without ads? What?! Christian Keil ("The Origin Story of Web 1.0 and 2.0," 2021) wrote:

> *"The internet was kept non-commercial through its early development. This gave developers the ability to build, test, experiment, scrap, and re-build their way to systems that worked at scale without financial pressure. This breathing room*

allowed for generations of tech development to pass before most consumers had even heard of the internet at all."

Let that settle in your mind for a minute—it's important. Think back to the original intent and consumerism. Clearly, great minds eventually went to work to figure out how to monetize the future of the web! The first banner ad finally popped up in 1994. It didn't take long.

As technology advanced, we moved from the library, one-way interaction of Web 1.0 to Web 2.0 and with new and improved social networking abilities. Interestingly, businesses weren't completely convinced that the internet and having a website would improve their bottom line or how people shopped. Web 2.0 eventually changed their minds.

Web 2.0: The Dawn of Interactivity and User-Generated Content

In 2004, O'Reilly Media coined the term "Web 2.0" to delineate the second generation of the WorldWideWeb, a new phase that emphasized web-based communities, user-generated content, and the capacity for users to interact with one another and exchange information seamlessly.

Web 2.0 revolutionized the way we perceived the internet, providing a significant leap forward in file storage and sharing capabilities. It wasn't just about reading or viewing content anymore; this era ushered in the potential for two-way interactions that transcended chat rooms, email, and photo sharing. Now users could post and share audio and video files, shop online, or even research service providers.

During the advent of Web 2.0, a debate flourished: "Do I need a website or not?" Remember, in the initial days, there were no ready-to-use web-page templates or DIY options for hosting a web page. It required a significant investment: hiring someone to write the code and then identifying a hosting service for your website. If you braved these new waters as an early adopter, your site probably resembled a one-page résumé with a couple of photographs. The fortunate ones would have hired someone who ensured the content was aligned and the photos were perfectly displayed. It was indeed the wild west of web development— certainly not always visually pleasing and a risky business expense filled with doubts.

This technological boom catalyzed the emergence of social networking sites. The year 2002 saw the launch of Friendster, initially envisioned as a dating site. Despite its immense popularity, Friendster ultimately succumbed to its own success—the site hadn't anticipated its sudden surge in popularity, and the server infrastructure simply couldn't keep up. As a result, users started to migrate to other emerging platforms for their social needs.

By 2003, LinkedIn, a platform targeting professionals and career-focused individuals, was launched. The same year also saw tech giant Google acquiring Blogger, a prominent blogging platform, and the debut of MySpace, which would become a defining social network of the Web 2.0 era.

In this period of remarkable innovation and exploration, Web 2.0 ushered in a whole new era of personalization and interaction on the internet. The pioneering social media platforms such as Friendster, LinkedIn, and MySpace set the stage for the explosion of user-generated content, reshaping the digital landscape.

One of the key aspects of this era was the emergence of blogs. Suddenly, people with an internet connection could share their thoughts, ideas, and experiences with the world. Platforms like Blogger made it easy to create and publish content, democratizing the creation and distribution of information. This, in turn, led to the birth of the modern influencer, as ordinary people gained the ability to amass large followings and shape public opinion.

In 2004, the social media landscape was forever changed with the launch of Facebook. Initially designed for college students, Facebook quickly expanded its user base and became the dominant social networking site. Unlike earlier platforms, Facebook allowed users to create a personal profile and connect with friends, family, and acquaintances in a more intimate setting. It also introduced innovative features such as the news feed and the Like button, which have since become staples of the social media experience.

Meanwhile, businesses began to recognize the potential of Web 2.0 to reach and engage with consumers. The static, one-page websites of the early days gave way to dynamic, interactive websites that allowed businesses to showcase their products, engage with customers, and even conduct transactions online.

As Web 2.0 evolved, we began to see the internet not just as a vast repository of information, but as a living, breathing community of users. This shift from static web pages to interactive platforms laid the foundation for the social media landscape as we know it today. However, even as we marveled at these advancements, new developments were on the horizon, hinting at yet another transformation of the digital world. As the saying goes, the only constant in technology is change, and the story of social media is no exception.

LinkedIn

Reflecting on the early days of social media, I remember my first encounter with LinkedIn, a platform that has certainly stood the test of time. It was around 2004, just a year after LinkedIn was launched, that I created my account on this professional networking site. I was looking for a way to connect with like-minded individuals in my industry, and LinkedIn seemed like a promising avenue.

As time passed, LinkedIn became more than just a site where I could upload my résumé and scroll through job listings. It started playing a significant role in my professional life. I began using LinkedIn to connect with colleagues, engage in insightful discussions, and even attend industry-specific events. It was through LinkedIn that I met one of my most influential mentors, a connection that has tremendously influenced my career trajectory.

Back in 2003, LinkedIn emerged as a pioneer, carving out a unique niche focusing on business and employment-oriented networking. Over the years, it has gracefully evolved from a simple résumé-posting site to a robust platform offering offline events, job posts, articles, and groups, and even multimedia posts.

Much like the popular "Six Degrees of Kevin Bacon" concept, LinkedIn uses degrees of connections to expand your professional network. The platform showcases your first-, second-, and third-level connections, fostering a sense of interconnectedness among professionals from varied industries.

However, just like any other large-scale platform, LinkedIn has faced its share of controversies, particularly concerning data usage and privacy. But despite these challenges, LinkedIn has proven its resilience and its immense value for professionals across the globe. Today, even high school students are hopping on LinkedIn to explore future prospects, further solidifying its staying power.

In the fast-paced world of social media, platforms come and go, constantly reinventing themselves in hopes of hitting the ever-shifting tastes of online audiences. Remember when MySpace once reigned supreme? For years the premier social hub, it has since evolved and taken on a niche role after Facebook's meteoric rise. Other sites like Friendster and GeoCities were left in the dust, relics of a bygone internet era.

Amidst this turbulent environment, LinkedIn has managed to steadily stay relevant and continue thriving. While its growth may have paled in comparison to Facebook, LinkedIn resisted overhauling itself to chase trends. It doubled down on its core value proposition – serving professionals. This relentless focus on business networking has allowed LinkedIn to adapt and expand without losing sight of its purpose.

Over 15 years since its launch, LinkedIn continues providing tangible value to its loyal user base. Its resilience speaks volumes about the platform's capacity to incrementally improve while still delivering on its original premise. Both professionals and recruiters turn to LinkedIn for connections and opportunities. While flashier networks have flared up and faded, LinkedIn prevails by evolving without forgetting its roots. Staying power derives from staying true to your core.

Indeed, LinkedIn's adaptability can be seen in the wide array of features it offers to foster professional relationships and connections. The endorsement and recommendation features, for instance, have transformed how we perceive professional credibility. As someone who's been on the platform for years, I can vouch for the value these features provide. Having received endorsements for my skills and recommendations from colleagues and employers, I've seen firsthand how they can elevate a professional profile.

However, it's essential to note that while LinkedIn offers an invaluable tool for professional networking and career advancement, it's not immune to the pitfalls associated with data management. The platform has been embroiled in several lawsuits over alleged data scraping and improper use of user profiles. Such issues serve as a reminder that the road to maintaining a successful social media platform is often rocky and fraught with legal and ethical challenges.

Despite these challenges, it's clear that LinkedIn has firmly established its place in the social media landscape. Its longevity and continued relevance are testaments to its ability to fulfill a unique need within the professional community.

As we move forward and explore the ever-evolving world of social media, I can't help but recall the early days of platforms like LinkedIn and MySpace. My journey with social media began with MySpace, a platform that, despite fading into the background, still holds a place of nostalgia in my heart. This nostalgia serves as a reminder of how far we've come in the realm of social media—and how much further we have to go.

As we delve deeper into the world of LinkedIn and other platforms that have made their mark, we'll continue to explore the transformations they've undergone, the challenges they've faced, and the impact they've had on our communication and connection in the digital age.

MySpace

Ah . . . MySpace. Launched in 2003, it was the pioneer of the modern social networking landscape. In its heyday, MySpace was a cultural phenomenon, a digital playground where users could customize their profiles, share music, and connect with friends.

MySpace was the FIRST global social networking site and the grandfather of sites and companies like YouTube. Yes, Tom in his white T-shirt was our first friend on the internet. It began as a file storage and personal profile site first used by employees at a company called "eUniverse." The company incentivized employees to sign up users by exploiting its 20 million email subscribers. This strategy ended with MySpace becoming the most popular global website at that time. MySpace quickly transitioned from a file storage platform to a social media networking site. Of course, it isn't like the robust platforms we are used to now, but at the time it was totally awesome.

I didn't waste any time learning how to interact with the site. At that time, I was working to get my radio career up and running. I attended a smaller school, and there was a website for college students called Facemash (yes, there was some branding done to the social media giant's original name, circa 2003). We will get to this one later. Anyway, Facemash didn't see my small college as good enough to join its platform. So I was all in on MySpace. Additionally, since I worked at the college radio station, one of my jobs was to get musicians to send us their music to play on the station, royalty-free.

I became a "connector" by using my radio career and MySpace page to connect bands with radio stations, helping bands get exposure. It worked, and it didn't take long for me to realize that MySpace and social media had an incredible way of connecting people at lightning speed. I saw this was the future.

Before you could blink an eye, bands and musicians flocked to MySpace after Napster collapsed under copyright lawsuits and went bankrupt. MySpace gave bands and musicians more control by directly connecting, building a community of loyal followers, and sharing music for free. At the time, it was revolutionary!

The president of MySpace, Chris DeWolfe, believed the same, because in 2005 he held talks with Mark Zuckerberg, hoping to acquire a little social platform called "The Facebook" (renamed in 2004). DeWolfe offered Zuckerberg $75 million. The race was on! Eventually, News Corporation beat out Viacom and purchased MySpace for a whopping $850 million. Everyone saw the social networking site as a way to monetize advertising and cross-advertise. Sound familiar?

At the height of MySpace's popularity in 2007, new users surpassed 320,000 registrations a day, with users viewing over 650 pages per month. Google took notice and negotiated the exclusive rights to sponsor links and web search results. The deal resulted in MySpace generating $30 million every month in revenue. Gone were the days of grassroots social connection, to be replaced by the days of big data and advertising!

In the meantime, Facebook had quietly been working its way into the mainstream.

Facebook

Facebook, launched in 2004, has undeniably shaped the landscape of social media as we know it today. It took over from MySpace as the leading social media platform by 2009, and my journey with Facebook, like that of many others, is a tale of adaptation and discovery.

I remember joining Facebook during its early days. The platform's focus on real identities and connections with people you actually knew was a sharp contrast to MySpace's culture. Facebook encouraged conversations and meaningful interactions and gave a new dimension to maintaining relationships. The thrill of reconnecting with old schoolmates and extended family members, coupled with the ease of sharing life updates, made Facebook incredibly appealing.

However, it wasn't always smooth sailing. Facebook faced its own set of challenges. By 2009, as it continued to expand and innovate, MySpace began to decline. It was argued that MySpace's fall was due to its focus on entertainment and media, owned as it was by News Corporation and with Viacom showing interest. The spirit of community began to take a back seat to advertising revenue.

As Facebook fostered a culture of improved social networking opportunities, MySpace became inundated with advertisements, making the site less flexible and slower. This change in dynamics is a crucial chapter in the history of social media. It demonstrates the importance of user experience and continual innovation, themes we'll continue to explore as we delve deeper into the evolution of social media.

While MySpace execs were grappling with corporate greed to push more advertising at the cost of user experience, Facebook pushed focus on the user—the community experience. While Facebook was founded in 2004, its popularity came with frustrated MySpace users migrating in 2007–2008. Facebook was officially no longer a college student platform and opened the gates to allow everyone to join. The platform had a steady migration, and there was a definite FOMO (fear of missing out) vibe at the time. Everybody wanted to know what all the buzz was about—and if you were young or "in the know," you were on the hottest ticket (platform) in town.

Facebook started as a website similar to Hot or Not called "Facemash." It was simply a photo comparison site where you would see two photos and choose who is "hot" or "not." If you are familiar with the Hot or Not application and appalled by it, you wouldn't be alone. Harvard forced the shutdown of the site and then threatened to expel Zuckerberg for the content. Zuckerberg was undeterred and switched gears, making the site a social study tool.

Back in the day, a "face book" was considered a student directory—historically, a paper version with student photos and information. Eventually, the "face book" landed on internal online directories. But Zuckerberg felt he could do it better and in less time. This, in turn, gave rise to "TheFacebook." And from there, you could say the rest was history.

Facebook became the most used social networking site. The "wall" feature allowed users to post messages, photos, and videos. Later, "tagging" allowed users to share and tag friends in photos. This seems elementary now, but back then if someone took a photo of you and you didn't have a camera, you had to ask the person to share it with you via email or head to the local drugstore to get it printed for you. Now it was as easy as a click of a button, and it would appear on your wall.

Of course, it didn't take big companies long to see the advertising potential. At first, it seemed harmless. Companies like Procter & Gamble did surveys on products and were able to have direct interactions with consumers. Not only that, but Facebook would announce changes users made to their page or products they purchased. As you can imagine or remember, that screamed invasion of privacy.

Facebook continues to struggle with maintaining the original intent of providing a place for community while finding a way to be profitable through monetization and consumerism. The platform seems to go through peaks and valleys where users are frustrated but cannot help but engage. Of course, when frustrated, users always Tweet their frustrations on X.

X/Twitter

X began as a simple microblogging service confined to 140 characters. The platform captured attention for its brevity and accessibility, letting users share thoughts and connect like one giant chatroom. But this simplicity left some users feeling overwhelmed, unable to get their voice heard in the busy stream.

When Elon Musk acquired X for $44 billion in 2022, he aimed to maximize the platform's potential while preserving its essence. First on the agenda was one small but significant shift – changing the name from Twitter to X. While met with some backlash, Musk defended the rebranding as a way to represent the unknown potential ahead. It symbolized innovation without losing the recognizable blue bird at its core.

Musk's purchase of Twitter in October 2022 shook the tech world. Some hoped the controversial billionaire would reinvigorate the stagnant platform. Others feared he would unravel Twitter's hard-won progress on safety and civility. After the deal closed, Musk got straight to work putting his mark on Twitter. His first major move was firing top executives like CEO Parag Agrawal and policy head Vijaya Gadde. He portrayed this as a clean slate to enact his vision.

True to his word, Musk rapidly introduced changes both small and seismic. The rebranding to X signaled a new direction. Features like X Blue subscriptions provided new revenue streams. But his boldest change targeted content moderation. Musk quickly criticized X's content rules as stifling free speech. He voiced plans to reform speech policies and unban suspended accounts. This sparked concerns of a rise in harassment, misinformation and extremism.

True to his word, Musk swiftly enacted a "general amnesty" reinstating banned accounts like Donald Trump's. He dismantled the trust and safety teams responsible for enforcing X's rules. Rules prohibiting COVID and election misinformation were scrapped.

Civil rights groups warned these moves could undermine years of hard-won safety measures on the site. But Musk insisted loosening restrictions would strengthen public debate and transparency. Only time will tell how this gamble plays out.

While Musk stirred controversy shaking up content rules, he was not the first to recognize X's unique potential for sparking real-time conversations. Twitter originally hit the digital scene in 2006 with its own convention-breaking approach.

The 140-character limit forced brevity, making Twitter the place for quick takes and up-to-the-second updates. This restriction shaped Twitter into a platform for concise commentary. Users could instantly share brief thoughts on events as they unfolded.

Where platforms like Facebook and MySpace were social directories, X focused on the right-now. Its core purpose was giving everyone a real-time microphone directly from the source. This focus on instant updates sets X apart.

My introduction to Twitter was somewhat accidental. I was skeptical initially, unsure of how meaningful conversations could be crafted within such a tight character limit. The concept of tweeting, retweeting, and hashtags seemed strange, but I decided to give it a try. My first few tweets were nothing more than daily life updates. But as time passed, I found myself increasingly drawn into the Twittersphere.

Twitter became my go-to platform for quick, real-time news updates and trend tracking. It was fascinating to observe how it transformed from a simple messaging platform into a significant hub for public discourse. And in a professional context, it allowed me to interact with thought leaders, industry peers, and even customers in a way that other platforms didn't.

The spontaneous, fast-paced nature of Twitter introduced a new dynamic to social media. Through hashtags, it offered a way for like-minded individuals to connect over shared interests and trending topics. This shift underscored the power of social media to bring people together in real time around shared experiences, ideas, and events, an aspect that still holds great importance in our digital communication today.

X has been hard to explain, but the best way to describe it is as status updates, or as the founder Jack Dorsey says, "a short burst of inconsequential information." I would argue that since his statement in 2006, the "inconsequential" isn't so anymore.

People like X for the sense of connectedness because you can follow celebrities and news as life happens and interact in the moment in short bursts. It's like fancy text messages that are broadcast to the world.

Twitter's origin story is kind of special. It actually started in 2006 as a side project for a podcasting company called "Odeo" (another one of my passions). The team working on the project came up with the idea for Twitter as a way to keep people updated on what was happening with the company in real time.

While X might seem like it's all about celebrity gossip and what people are eating for lunch, it's actually used for a lot of different things. For example, many news organizations use X to share stories and breaking news. Politicians also use X to connect with constituents and get their message out there.

Perhaps one of the most significant contributions X made to social media and how we use it is the hashtag—#. We see hashtags everywhere now. But that wasn't always the case. It started with Chris Messina in 2007. He was trying to find a solution for Twitter's need for "some kind of group organizing framework." Initially, he was laughed out of the room—it would be too "nerdy" and would never work. He didn't listen. Instead, he asked a friend to try it in real time when tweeting about a wildfire, and it caught on like—well, like wildfire. By 2009, Twitter added it as a way to search for topics of interest. By 2010, Instagram users started hashtagging, and in 2013 Facebook adopted hashtags.

Of course, businesses are always trying to figure out how to monetize and advertise. So if you are trying to get away from social media ads, you won't find comfort here. But the good news is as a business, you can work to promote organically through tweets or through promoted ads.

X and Facebook have both come under scrutiny over the years for different reasons. I won't dive into the mess because I believe all social media can be used for good. It's all about the mindset and the future!

That brings us to Instagram!

Instagram

Instagram came on the scene in 2010, and it quickly became one of the most popular social media platforms. It was originally designed as a photo- and video-sharing app, and users could post pictures and add tags to them. The app was initially known as "Burbn," inspired by the founder Kevin Systrom's love of fine whiskey and bourbons. Systrom had worked at Google and interned at Odeo (later X).

I remember when I first downloaded Instagram on my smartphone. At the time, I was just fascinated with the ability to transform my everyday snapshots into works of art with just a tap of a filter. It felt creative and fun, and it was easy to share these edited images with my friends and family.

As an avid traveler, I quickly made Instagram my virtual photo album. I loved that I could share my adventures with others in such a visual and immersive way. I found myself spending more and more time exploring the app, not just posting my own content but also engaging with other people's content.

Soon I started to see the true power of Instagram as a tool for personal branding and business marketing. Brands, influencers, and even small businesses were using the platform to visually tell their stories, connect with their audiences, and even sell products directly.

The key difference in Instagram's early days was that the platform focused exclusively on photos taken with a mobile device. Systrom and his team wanted to bridge the gap between photo apps like Hipstamatic and Facebook. One was great at photos; the other was great at social media and sharing.

Instagram seemed like a good mash-up of Facebook sharing, X-like short posts, and the photo capabilities and features of Hipstamatic. The name "Instagram" came about when Systrom decided to focus on the instant telegram.

Of course, the rest is history. The app was launched and ended the first day with 25,000 users. It only took a few short months to reach 1 million users. And before its initial public offering, Facebook swooped in and bought the company for $1 billion. At the time of the purchase, Instagram is said to have had 27 million users.

Fast-forward a few years, and when it felt like Facebook and X became overrun with ads and social division over politics and neighborhood fights, Insta stepped in as a safe haven. Younger generations decided they had enough with Boomers and the shenanigans and migrated. Instagram's direct messaging (DM) became popular. Part of pop culture was "sliding into someone's DMs"—for older generations, Instagram expanded the urban dictionary. The slang expanded to include #TBT (Throwback Thursday), #FoodPorn, and #Regram—the list goes on!

Instagram was also a little more creative. Unlike Facebook and X, Instagram offered photo filters and editing and the ability to geotag photos. Over time, Instagram has evolved to include other features, such as storytelling, live—and, of course, ads. In recent years, Instagram has also become a place where people can share their creative content, such as music and dance videos. Today, Instagram is used by millions of people around the world to connect with friends, share their lives, and express themselves creatively. The platform isn't going away. As a matter of fact, it keeps finding ways to evolve to compete with newcomers. So we should learn how to work within the system, right?! That brings me to TikTok!

TikTok

Yet another social media platform to navigate, yay! Or no?

Do you remember Musical.ly? Or Vine? They were popular photo- and video-sharing apps until 2018. Then Musical.ly was bought by a Chinese company, and Musical.ly users were migrated over to what is now known as TikTok.

TikTok is a photo- and video-streaming app that gives you photo filters, music, sounds, and editing options to create personalized videos that you can share and post. The difference from other platforms is the localization of the content and interaction even though it is a global application. Challenges and contests are created based on location.

To be honest, when I first heard about TikTok, I was a little skeptical. As a seasoned social media user, I wasn't sure if I was ready for yet another platform, especially one that seemed to be so different from anything else out there. However, as I started to hear more about it from friends and colleagues, curiosity got the best of me, and I decided to give it a try.

The moment I opened TikTok, it felt like I was stepping into a whole new world. The short, catchy videos, the incredible creativity of the users, and the contagious energy of the platform pulled me in immediately. I found myself scrolling through endless videos, laughing at comedic skits, getting inspired by innovative DIYs, learning from educational clips, and even attempting a few dance challenges myself.

One thing I particularly appreciate about TikTok is its ability to discover and promote new talent. Unlike other platforms where users often need to have a sizable following to gain visibility, TikTok's algorithm gives anyone the chance to go viral, which I believe is a big part of its appeal.

From a professional perspective, I quickly realized the potential of TikTok for business and marketing. Brands can truly let their hair down and show a more human side through fun, engaging content. It's a refreshing break from the polished aesthetic that has become prevalent on other social media platforms.

The platform is fairly easy to use and has quickly gained popularity. During the pandemic, TikTok was a lifeline to younger people who found themselves isolated from human interaction. It brought a sense of connectedness and joy to everyone during social distancing.

But, of course, with popularity comes the need to capitalize. However, while you will find ads on TikTok, as of this writing, the ads aren't as invasive as on other platforms like Facebook. If you don't like the ad that pops up, you can simply continue scrolling through your feed. How you are fed ads and videos is based on algorithms. TikTok algorithms are like no other—they are revolutionary, and that is why so many people have flocked to the platform.

You can also find specific videos based on your current curiosity;

you need to use the search tool. There are entire sections dedicated to different interests. There is a CleanTok, BookTok, BabyTok, Recipes of TikTok—the list goes on and on. For now, the Toks are more community-centered. And that is the key!

Controversies Surrounding TikTok

Despite its meteoric rise and global popularity, TikTok has found itself mired in controversy. Concerns over national security, data privacy, and content regulation have led to outright bans in several countries, including India, the United States, and the United Kingdom.

TikTok, owned by Chinese tech giant ByteDance, has triggered national security fears in various regions. The perceived risk is rooted in the suspicion that the Chinese government might access user data for intelligence purposes. This apprehension led the US government to ban TikTok downloads on government-issued devices in 2020.

Data Privacy and Content Concerns

The data privacy practices of TikTok have also come under scrutiny. The platform amasses a plethora of user data including location information, biometric data, and browsing history, stored on servers in the United States and China. Many fear that this data might be misused by the app owners or the Chinese government.

Concerns also arise regarding the nature of content allowed on TikTok. The platform has faced criticism for permitting videos promoting violence, hate speech, and dangerous challenges. It was such content concerns that led the Taliban government in Afghanistan to ban TikTok for leading youth astray.

TikTok's Response and the Uncertain Future

TikTok has staunchly denied all these allegations.

The company asserts that it neither shares user data with the Chinese government nor neglects data privacy. It also vows to remove harmful content from the platform. Despite these assurances, the bans persist, leaving a cloud of uncertainty over TikTok's future in several countries.

The question of whether TikTok could be banned for all Americans looms large. If national security and data privacy concerns persist, and if harmful content continues to appear on the platform, the US government may take a more definitive stand against the app. Despite TikTok's efforts to address these concerns, a precedent exists for the US government banning apps deemed threatening to national security or public safety. Thus the possibility of an outright ban on TikTok cannot be ruled out.

To TikTok or Not to TikTok?

Whether to continue using TikTok is an individual decision, influenced by a range of factors. Data privacy and national security concerns might prompt some users to delete the app. For others, disturbing content might be the deciding factor. However, if you enjoy the platform and aren't particularly troubled by these concerns, there's no imperative reason to abandon TikTok.

The choice ultimately hinges on personal judgment. It involves weighing the risks against the benefits of using the app and making a decision aligned with your personal comfort and values.

* * *

For every social media platform or application, the rise in popularity can be credited to driving and building that sense of community and connectedness. However, despite that, each is driven toward a path of consumerism.

If there was a way to find a balance between consumerism and authentic human interaction, what would it look like?

I'm so glad you asked—I think it can be found in Web3 or the metaverse!

Chapter 4

Embracing the Future: Web3 and the Metaverse

Navigating through the continuously evolving world of digital communication can feel like a never-ending journey. Just when you're feeling at home with familiar platforms like Zoom and Facebook, something new surfaces. I can almost hear your sighs! But let's take a moment to imagine this: What if Web3 and the metaverse held the potential to craft a more authentic, personalized, and interconnected digital experience? Suddenly, the prospect becomes less daunting and more enticing, doesn't it? This chapter explores these possibilities and much more. As we delve into Web3 and the metaverse, remember, every new wave of technology offers us incredible opportunities to enhance the way we communicate and connect.

Explain It to Me Like I'm a Fifth Grader

Web3 is an umbrella term for a set of emerging technologies that aim to provide a more interactive and personal experience on the web. These include things like virtual reality, augmented reality, artificial intelligence, and blockchain technology.

Chances are you know virtual reality or augmented reality. It is already being used in some gaming applications and is becoming more popular all the time. Think Oculus! In the commercial, if you spent any time looking at houses online, you may have come across the 3D house tour. For those, you have the option of using your headset, or you can use the arrow keys on your keyboard to walk through the house. You can look up and down and side to side.

But what about the other technologies?

Artificial intelligence is a field of computer science that deals with making computers "smart"—that is, being able to understand complex tasks and carry out humanlike reasoning. This could be used to create more personalized experiences on websites or even to help you find the information you didn't even know you were looking for yet! Yes, on the consumer side, there are the usual concerns over invading privacy, but those concerns are based on Web 2.0 technology. In Web3, privacy becomes enhanced by using blockchain technology.

Blockchain technology is best known for its use in cryptocurrencies like Bitcoin, but it has many other potential uses. Essentially, it is a way of storing data in a decentralized manner so that it is secure and tamperproof. For example, Web 2.0 stores information in one central location, usually on a company's server in a data center. Alternatively, blockchain could be used to create a new kind of internet, where data is stored on a global network of computers instead of on central servers. Blockchain is similar to the decentralization of Web 1.0, where data is (and was) peer-to-peer. Back then, your information went from you to the server of the business or person on the other end.

With Web 2.0, data is owned by the entity to which you give it. Facebook, LinkedIn, TikTok—as soon as you put your data on the platform, it's theirs through the terms of use or terms of service agreements we accept but never read. In Web3, the idea is that you take back ownership of your data, which can't be stored or used by these platforms or websites without specific permission.

The Metaverse

"Metaverse" is a term that was first coined by science fiction writer Neal Stephenson in his novel Snow Crash. It refers to a virtual world that is populated by avatars—that is, digital representations of real people. This differs from the current crop of virtual worlds like Second Life, which are populated by computer-generated characters.

The metaverse could be thought of as a kind of 3D internet, where users can interact with each other in a more realistic way and even carry out transactions using virtual currency. Some believe that the metaverse will eventually replace the physical world as our primary reality. Of course, that is up for debate, but it is about thinking into the future.

Web3 vs. the Metaverse

Some people use the terms "Web3" and "metaverse" interchangeably, but they are actually two different things. The metaverse is a specific vision of the future that includes a virtual world populated by avatars. At the same time, Web3 is a more general term that refers to the next generation of the internet.

So what's the difference? Well, the metaverse is just one possible application of Web3 technologies. It's an ambitious and far-reaching vision, but it's not the only thing for which Web3 can be used. For example, other applications of these technologies include decentralized applications (dApps), distributed ledger technology (DLT), and unhosted web applications. I won't go into the weeds on these because then we have to talk about the banks, and money, and tech that can be hard to wrap your head around.

The key takeaway for social media is that while the metaverse is just one possible future for the internet, Web3 is a broader term that refers to the next generation of the internet as a whole.

Why Should You Care About Web3 and the Metaverse?

There are a few reasons why you might want to pay attention to these developments:

1. They could change the way we interact with the internet. Web3 and the metaverse are becoming a reality. As business owners, we adapt or get left behind! Both could change the way we use the internet entirely. Imagine being able to step into a virtual world and explore it just like you would the real world. Or being able to buy things using virtual currency. Consider the fashion industry, for instance. As a business owner in this field, think of the advantages of virtual fitting rooms for you and your customers. Instead of your customers clicking through a flat catalog of dresses on a website, imagine them walking into your virtual store, picking up a 3D representation of a dress, and trying it on their virtual avatar. Payments, too, could be revolutionized with the incorporation of blockchain technology, using cryptocurrencies for instant, secure transactions.

2. Web3 and the metaverse could make the internet more personal. Imagine a world where the websites you visit are tailored specifically to you. That personalized future is what Web3 and metaverse technologies could enable. Today, we all see the same generic content online—it's a one-size-fits-all experience. But Web3 may revolutionize digital interactions by customizing them to each user.

Take buying tickets as an example. Currently, ticketing sites display the same seating options to every visitor. But imagine a customized system where you log in and see seat selections personalized for you. If you like cheaper seats, budget sections are highlighted. If your friend prefers closer seats, premium options are prominently featured instead.

This exemplifies the more curated, individualized experiences that

Web3 could create. Companies may finally understand customers' unique preferences and showcase content catered specifically to them. The internet would feel less like a static webpage and more like an engaging experience designed just for you.

The result? You may feel more valued, while businesses boost engagement and sales. Web3 brings the promise of tailored digital interactions that feel personal, not generic. The future internet may be shaped around you.

Now I know there have been issues with Facebook and selling information without consent. We all see ads based on purchases made from other sites not attached to Facebook. We have all experienced having a conversation with someone and waking up to ads on our feed based on that conversation. I admit it is a little creepy. But here's the thing. Web3 addresses that by putting the power back in your hands. You will be able to choose what information you share and with whom. You will be able to opt out of certain features if you want to. In other words, in Web3 you will have control over your own data!

3. The metaverse and Web3 could have a significant impact on businesses. Virtual reality and augmented reality are already being used by some businesses, but the applications are only just scratching the surface. Web3 and the metaverse are becoming a reality and opening up a whole new world of possibilities for businesses of all kinds.

From retail to education to healthcare, metaverse technologies have the potential to disrupt entire industries. In the logistics industry, augmented reality is already improving warehouse operations. One client in California provided workers with smart glasses that efficiently guided them to correct product locations, reducing pull errors to virtually zero.

Now imagine if your business could implement a similar digital enhancement. Employees could wear augmented reality headsets that visually direct them around the warehouse. The headsets would use overlays of arrows and highlighted objects to guide the worker to the needed items among the shelves and racks. This real-time spatial guidance could significantly reduce mistakes in retrieving items, as the California company discovered.

The metaverse enables these kinds of immersive, productivity-boosting applications across sectors. For logistics and warehousing specifically, augmented reality offers the next evolution in organization and accuracy by providing visual orientation. The possibilities for digital tech to transform traditional business operations are only growing.

4. If the internet becomes more immersive and realistic, it could have a big impact on the way we live our lives. We could start spending more time in virtual worlds and less time in the physical world. Or we could use augmented reality to enhance our everyday experiences. I believe the core of engagement will remain— tailored content that educates, entertains, and fosters community. This principle anchors my four-post approach detailed later.

Yes, there are concerns over younger generations spending too much time on phones, social media, and games. Personally, I've seen how this technology can bridge gaps in our personal lives. My family is spread out across different states, but through the metaverse, we've been able to gather together for a game night, just like old times. We could interact in a 3D virtual living room, mimicking the feel of being together in one place. This same principle could be applied to virtual team-building events in a business context. If you have a new product, you can do a 3D presentation or host a meeting in 3D. It would be Zoom on steroids and less clunky than the dreaded video with chat windows.

5. It's not just a pie-in-the-sky future vision—Web3 and the metaverse are already starting to take shape. These aren't distant, futuristic ideas. In fact, one of my clients, a tech start-up, has already begun experimenting with blockchain for its internal operations and customer transactions. It's finding new ways to incorporate Web3 technologies into its business model, which is propelling the company ahead of its competitors. This is just one example of how these technologies are gradually shaping our present. So it's definitely something to warm up to.

* * *

You still have time as everyone is tinkering with the possibilities. So, for now, you need to make sure you are leveraging the current Web 2.0 social media platforms in the most effective ways possible. This way, you will be ready for the changes and be an early adopter!

Chapter 5

Leveraging Web 2.0 for the Future

Before we delve into the dynamic potential of the existing social media platforms, let's take a moment to reflect on our current practices. What narrative is your social media presence currently weaving about you? There's a good chance that many of you are already harnessing its power quite impressively. And for those feeling a bit less confident, don't worry!

The truth is, we're all doing our best navigating the ever-evolving realm of social media, but it's only natural to encounter a few stumbling blocks along the way. Let's keep in mind, creating a compelling and impactful online presence isn't a matter of luck—it's about thoughtful planning and strategy. And remember, no matter where you're starting from, there's always room to learn, grow, and refine your approach!

First things first, do you have personal social media and/or professional or business social media accounts? Take a look at your profiles—I'll wait. Now what I usually see are two things. On the one hand, people will have a personal page where they (maybe) sprinkle business posts among posts of where and what they ate or posts of their kids, pets, weddings, or other family events. In one way, you are letting your community get to know you personally. However, it might be a little too personal.

On the other hand, I see others with personal and business profiles. Yay! However, the business profile collects dust with very few posts or posts that fail to connect with the viewer at a personal level. Sometimes it is all third-person testimonials or personal accomplishments. Other times it is stock posts automatically posted by a third-party company. Rarely do I see engaging posts that will draw people in and pique their curiosity.

In other words, if you are posting random cat, food, kid, wedding photos and videos—they should connect to what you do as a business. If not, keep those on your personal page and have a separate business page. That is step one. From there, shift focus and integrate your social media with a higher purpose.

I won't pretend that social media doesn't take work; it does—and a lot of it! But don't let that scare you off or get you frustrated. Having a plan and strategy will help make it easier. To begin, think community—not sales, likes, or followers.

Watch the Trends

Whether your social media engagement is personal or strictly business-focused, keeping abreast of trends is crucial. The essence of social media is being in tune with what's happening at the very moment, the NOW. To forge a deeper connection with your audience, maintaining relevance is key, and achieving relevance involves keeping your finger on the pulse of what people are currently drawn to, then capitalizing on it most effectively on each platform.

For instance, do you remember when Instagram introduced Instagram Reels? This exciting feature offered a fresh, dynamic way to share content, but did you harness its power? Are you using it now? And what about Facebook Stories? As a personal example, when I first integrated these tools into my content strategy, I noticed a significant increase in both views and engagement across my Instagram and Facebook accounts. It wasn't just a matter of users consuming more content; it was also about audiences engaging more deeply with the brand. In fact, a survey by Facebook IQ found that "62% of people said they became more interested in a brand or product after seeing it in a story."

These shifts aren't confined to Instagram and Facebook; they permeate throughout various platforms. X, for instance, introduced social audio rooms. LinkedIn has focused on supporting creators by offering a way to grow their email lists via newsletters. Even Amazon has hopped onto the trend train with live video.

So how do you stay current with these trends? It's about being observant and proactive. Set aside time to explore different platforms and features, sign up for newsletters that cover social media trends, and listen to relevant podcasts. Don't be afraid to experiment with new features and formats—this is how I discovered the potential of Instagram Reels and Facebook Stories! Pay attention to what is catching your audience's attention and where the conversation is heading. Staying informed and adaptable will ensure you're always one step ahead in the vibrant, ever-evolving world of social media.

Mind the Media

Another bit of advice is to consider your audience for each platform and the types of media you use. For example, longer videos are better on Facebook. Whereas content on Instagram and TikTok should be shorter. LinkedIn is better for short articles or blog posts. And X favors short links due to character limits.

Each platform also has a vibe. For example, think of Facebook as a family barbeque or reunion. Personally, you are interacting with people of all ages, and people often share family updates and photos. You want to engage at the family barbeque level, including PG-rated messages that mirror the user's and the platform's tone.

Instagram is like the club scene. You are interacting with a younger crowd with makeup and hair done, the perfect look, and a deliberate statement. It's like walking through the bar where everyone is peacocking for attention.

Then there is LinkedIn. LinkedIn is a professional networking event. Business-to-business casual conversations, no children, and everyone stays well mannered. People are looking to either build their professional network or learn about trends in their industry. You want to post accordingly.

Another central platform is X. This network is like a Hollywood free-for-all, though I exaggerate slightly. Politicians and celebrities mingle with everyday users. Many are just there to people watch, observing without actively posting.

The keys to success on X are twofold. First, avoid getting trapped in political divisions. Second, embrace the platform's short, creative nature. While X has struggled at times, it retains value for real-time news and connecting around shared interests.

However, some trends that previously boosted X have since faded. The hype around NFTs and Web3 that reenergized the platform has cooled significantly in recent months. The promised NFT X community relying on hashtags and conversations never fully materialized as interest waned.

But X continues evolving under its new owner, Elon Musk. It remains unique for accessing breaking news as it unfolds. And it connects people around specific topics and events without needing extensive networks. X still offers an unfiltered perspective if you know how to filter through the noise.

And, of course, there is TikTok. What started out as a Gen Z–focused platform then morphed into the social media mall. You have grandmas and grandpas power walking while they give advice on gardening and window-shop BookTok. Then there are adults looking for easy recipes, work-from-home and side-hustle strategies, and gift ideas and posting about social justice causes while at the food court. Finally, you have the younger generations with an innate need for shock and awe challenges and general pranks. You may also be sucked into the Sephora makeup tutorials. They run in and out by posting everything from "truth or dare" to fashion trends, pets, and cars. It can be busy!

Maintain Activity Without The Overwhelm

It's crucial to remember that maintaining an active social media presence doesn't have to lead to becoming overwhelming. In fact, it really boils down to leveraging the kind of media that resonates with you and tailoring your message to your specific audience. The golden rule here is to stay active—but let me clarify what that truly means.

When I say "stay active," I don't mean to imply that you need to inundate your feed with 10 posts every single day in order to get noticed or boost your engagement. In my experience, effective social media engagement isn't necessarily about quantity. In fact, it's about authentic interaction and connection.

One of the practical ways I apply this principle is through direct messages. Responding to DMs promptly and genuinely shows the people in your audience that you are present, approachable, and truly interested in their input or inquiries. For instance, when a customer reached out to me with a question about a product, I responded swiftly and personally. This resulted in not only a successful sale but also the development of a long-term customer relationship.

Being an active participant in the wider social media community can also make a significant difference. I make it a point to leave supportive or encouraging comments on other accounts, sharing thoughts or sparking conversation. I've found that this builds a sense of camaraderie and mutual support in the online sphere, further enhancing my social media presence.

Always remember the roots of social media: It was designed around the concept of communication and connection, of sparking conversation and building relationships. It was never meant to be a one-sided broadcast channel, solely for pushing products or services. So keep it social, keep it authentic, and keep the conversation going.

Focus on the Customer Experience

Another thing to consider is customer service. Social media is a great way to talk directly to customers, find out what they are looking for, and listen to them. Epictetus, a Greek philosopher, said, "You have two ears and one mouth so that we can listen twice as much as we speak." For social media, there is no better advice.

Customers want to be heard. Have you ever wondered why customers will more quickly voice a complaint and why trying to get a compliment is like pulling teeth sometimes? It comes down to wanting their grievance heard. We can learn a lot from a complaint. We can learn even more when we reach out beforehand. Use social media for research and development!

Keep a keen eye on your network, engagement, interactions, and outcomes. Thankfully, there's a multitude of tools available to aid you in tracking your social media performance. Even better, these tools can take on some of the more time-consuming tasks like researching hashtags, tracking trends, and collating other analytical data points.

In addition to this, there are tools that can assist you in creating social media templates and calendars for automating your post publishing. Commonly used ones include Buffer, Hootsuite, and Sprout Social, to name a few. But personally, I have a special fondness for Loomly, Metricool, and Flick. These tools, with their unique features and user-friendly interfaces, have proved to be invaluable in my social media management strategy.

If you haven't heard of Loomly, Metricool, or Flick, they are social media management tools. They are each a little different, but I use these because each has some cool features.

Loomly

Meet Loomly, a game changer in the realm of social media management that I've come to greatly appreciate. Why, you ask? It's all about streamlining your workflow and making social media marketing as straightforward as possible.

With Loomly, you can manage all your social media platforms in one convenient location. Its ability to suggest content ideas based on current trends, noteworthy events, and established best practices is an invaluable resource for content creation.

Notifications are another useful feature; you'll get alerts when someone comments on a post or when your team contributes to the account. This way, you stay connected with your audience and on top of all account activities.

But that's not all. Loomly's content scheduling feature is a real game changer. You can meticulously plan your social media calendar to automatically disseminate your content across all platforms—including your Google Business Profile. Yes, this includes ads as well!

And when it comes to performance assessment, Loomly's robust analytics tool has you covered. It enables you to measure the success of your posts and ads, giving you valuable insights into which topics or types of content resonate most with your audience.

Now all these excellent features do come with a price tag. However, Loomly offers a free trial to let you explore its potential. As of this writing, it offers a basic account for a very reasonable $26 per month, which covers two users and ten social media accounts. It's a small investment for an impactful start! If you're interested, you can sign up using my affiliate code at www.katiebrinkley.com/loomly. This won't cost you anything extra but will support me in continuing to share valuable insights with you.

One of my other favorites is Flick.

Flick.social

Overwhelmed by the prospect of leveraging the full potential of Instagram, Facebook, or TikTok? Flick might just be your savior. Born as a specialized toolset for Instagram, Flick has since expanded its services to accommodate Facebook and TikTok as well.

Similar to Loomly, Flick furnishes a content scheduler, permitting you to map out a full month of content in advance and have it auto-posted on specified dates and times. This feature is an absolute time-saver and allows you to maintain a consistent presence on your channels even during your busiest periods.

One area where Flick distinctively stands out is its powerful hashtag research tool. Hashtags can be the lifeblood of your posts on platforms like Instagram, guiding them to the right audiences. With Flick's tool, you can discover, manage, and critically analyze which hashtags are bolstering your reach and which ones are falling short. This knowledge empowers you to continually refine your hashtag strategy, maximizing your engagement and reach.

To help users effectively navigate the platform and make Instagram management less daunting, Flick provides comprehensive training and handy templates. Whether you're a seasoned Instagram pro or a newcomer, these resources can offer valuable insights to elevate your strategy.

Now it's worth mentioning that Flick isn't a free service. However, like Loomly, it does provide a free trial period. This gives you the chance to take it for a spin and see firsthand how it can enhance your social media management. As an affiliate for Flick, I am thrilled to offer you a direct link to get started. You can visit www.katiebrinkley.com/flick and by doing this you'll be on your path to simpler and more efficient social media management in no time!

Make the Time

Once you've zeroed in on your audience, determined the appropriate tone, chosen the media type, and crafted your message, it's time to commit. I often hear about time constraints from professionals juggling various responsibilities.

However, once your strategy is in place, it's merely a matter of developing a routine and sticking to it.

A haphazard approach, essentially throwing content at the wall to see what sticks, isn't just ineffective; it's a time sink. Consistency and adherence to your messaging strategy will foster the know-like-trust factor, gradually building your community and attracting brand advocates.

Consider your current social media habits. Are you spending an hour or more each day aimlessly scrolling? Imagine the productivity boost if even half that time were dedicated to executing a well-devised plan. Social media is a tool to be leveraged, not a burdensome obligation.

One practical approach is to batch-create your content. For instance, one of my clients dedicates the first Monday of each month to planning and creating all her posts for the upcoming weeks. She then schedules these posts using a scheduling tool like Loomly. This approach frees up her daily schedule, allowing her to focus on engaging with her audience.

Another method is to make the most of user-generated content (UGC). Sharing reviews, testimonials, and photos or videos shared by your community not only can save time but also can contribute to building authenticity and trust.

However, if time constraints are still an issue, outsourcing is an effective solution. By hiring a social media manager or a virtual assistant, you can ensure your social media presence is maintained without sacrificing your other commitments.

When outsourcing, be sure to look for a professional who understands your industry, has a clear strategy, and can demonstrate expertise with past successes. For example, I had a client in the health and wellness industry who outsourced his social media management to an agency unfamiliar with the sector. The generic content produced didn't resonate with the client's audience, and engagement rates dropped. When the client switched to a specialist in health and wellness social media, his engagement rates not only recovered but soared to new heights.

* * *

Remember, planning, strategy, and consistency are key in the realm of social media. With the right approach, you can make it a powerful tool rather than a consuming obligation.

And as I noted above, if you examine your time and truly feel you are too busy and don't have the time or patience to attend to a social media strategy, you can always outsource it. That's why I am here! I know that sometimes it is worth the price to outsource a job. Social media is not an exception. I admit there is a learning curve. Maybe you have the time to create the posts but struggle with the strategy. I can help with that too!

It's important to know that it's not too late to get started. If you focus on a strategy and plan now, you can explore ways to maximize each platform without reinventing the wheel.

Chapter 6

Best Strategies for Social Media

Now that you know that each platform has a little different vibe overall, it's essential to know what type of strategy works best for each platform. It's all about engagement and building community. You need to know where your target audience is and then use that platform.

The Social Media Calendar

Now let's talk about consistency, which is best achieved by creating a social media calendar. What's a social media calendar, you ask? It's a visual workflow that outlines what and when you'll post on different platforms. It's your strategic plan laid out on a calendar, which can be anything from a specialized tool to a whiteboard, a Google Calendar, or even a spreadsheet.

A well-structured social media calendar ensures that you map out your posts across different platforms and keep track of when to post them. But it doesn't end there. It also serves as a reminder to interact and engage with other accounts, enhancing your online presence.

Incorporating this into your daily routine will keep your social media activities from being overlooked or forgotten. There are plenty of ready-to-use social media calendar templates available online, saving you the hassle of starting from scratch. Remember, achieving success on social media is about having effective systems in place!

And to help you get started, I'd love to share a social media content calendar that I've personally crafted. You can download it from www.katiebrinkley.com/contentcalendar. Not only does it provide you with a solid foundation for planning your posts, but it also illustrates the kind of strategy I use for my own social media management. Please note that you'll need to provide your email address to access this resource. It's a small investment of your time for a valuable tool that can significantly enhance your social media productivity!

Some great places to look at different social media calendars can be found on Loomly, Flick, Trello, and even Canva. Once you have a calendar you like, do a brain dump by making a list. You want to list out current events, content you want to create, your needs, and photos or graphics you use. Keep it relevant! Is there a holiday around the corner? Special event? Do you have a newsletter or blog you want to share?

From there, it's all about plugging into the calendar! Put your content into buckets to organize your posts. Consider timing. For example, people LOVE mood boosters on Mondays. Pay attention to when your audience is engaged. What time of day is it? Are there some days they are more responsive than others? Then add variety, and space your content out. For instance, if you like doing quotes, do those on Monday for Motivation Monday. Remember Throwback Thursday? It worked, right?! Eventually, the trend took off, and everyone was posting bad senior photos. Why did it catch on? Because it was about community.

Maybe your calendar is Motivation Monday, Taco Tuesday, What About Wednesday—you get the idea. Be creative and thoughtful. Make it fun!

Finally, consider if the content will be cross-posted on Facebook and

Instagram or posted on Facebook only. Remember that not all content works across all platforms, and your audience might be on one but not another.

Now that you have the basics, let's dive into specific strategies for different platforms.

Facebook Strategies

Facebook seems like the easiest place to start. After all, it is still the most widely used and universal platform. You can post links, videos, articles, and stories of almost any length. Facebook is fairly easy to use, and even though younger people may focus on Instagram, the two platforms still remain connected—and Facebook and Instagram will cross-post to each other. Two birds, one stone!

Facebook presents a fantastic arena for branding, customer service, and sales, essentially functioning as a one-stop shop for businesses. The platform's wide array of features, from posts and ad campaigns to promotional activities, facilitates gaining a strong following and enhancing visibility. However, the magic lies in the QUALITY of your content, not the quantity.

Instead of flooding your followers' feeds with incessant posts, focus on delivering valuable, high-quality content. Consistency is crucial, but it doesn't mean you have to post several times a day. In fact, it's about regularity and a steady presence rather than frequency of posting. Heard otherwise? It's a common misconception. The true power of Facebook marketing lies in consistent delivery of compelling content that resonates with your audience.

Here's the thing. It used to be post, post, post. The advice was to post multiple times a day. However, the Facebook algorithms changed. The users complained that it was all business and advertising, so Facebook worked to try and get back to the "friends and family" feel of its past. With that, business interactions on news feeds fell. Now it is about authentic interaction and shareable content—and videos or links are often the keys!

Think about quality and what will move someone to SHARE what you post. You want to either solve a problem for, educate, or entertain the onlooker. When you provide something of value, you are able to connect and speak to your followers. This is how you build community.

Speaking of community—one of the most effective ways to find new clients and nurture your current clients is through Facebook Groups. Not convinced? You might want to reconsider. It is guessed that Zuckerberg invested as much as $11 million in the 2020 Super Bowl for two ads promoting Facebook Groups. The ad was part of Facebook's "More Together" campaign—you know—get back to community. The point is, Facebook is working and spending big money on Facebook Groups—so we need to consider the thought of embracing them.

Have you thought about creating a Facebook Group for your business? A group is a great place to talk about your product or service, answer questions, network and connect people, or offer sneak peeks, previews, and discounts. Of course, if this all sounds too overwhelming, search for Facebook Groups that you can join where members of the group would be your ideal client or customer. You can always start by interacting with comments and posts in that group. Then once you are comfortable, branch out! Branch out to other groups—and other platforms!

Instagram Strategies

Now before I say it—promise you will stick with me—Instagram Reels.

Instagram Reels

I know—I can hear you moan from here. But listen, Reels are it and can help you gain traction faster than posting random photos. Reels are designed to pick up on and follow the hottest trends. Combined with the right hashtags and captions, you will be unstoppable. Instagram Reels are a great way of creating content for your "Awareness" posts using the four-post methodology I'll outline soon.

Before jumping headfirst into Reels, I suggest doing an Instagram audit to optimize what you already have. It doesn't have to be painful, but it does need to be pointed out. Here is what you need to know when it comes to Instagram:

- **Know your "why."** What is the purpose of the Instagram account?

- **Update your profile.** "One and done" is not the profile you want to publish. What has changed?

- **Brand consistency.** Do you have a style or a mash-up of random posts?

- **What works.** Look at past content. Is it visually appealing? What post gained traction?

- **Captions.** Do they match your style, and are they well written to match your brand?

- **Hashtags.** What are you using that works? Niche, location, or community tags make a difference. Look—for everyone with less than 100,000 followers, hashtags STILL work to get more reach when you use them the right way.

- **Reciprocation.** Are you engaged with other accounts or followers? It is a two-way street.

- **Timing.** Posting schedules matter! You need to post when followers are active on the platform.

- **Bots.** Are fake accounts or bots following you? Clean house! These followers can hurt you.

- **Research.** Check your competitors for their following, imagery, ads, and keywords.

We find that more and more brands are coming to us to get a second pair of eyes to help with the audit. This makes sense, as it will help to remove any cognitive bias from your audit.

Consider getting a trusted peer to help you with this, or reach out to me and my team; we would love to help.

The Hashtag

Now let's talk hashtags. With all the changes, one thing still remains essential to Instagram, and that is the hashtag. Hashtags are still one of the best tools, and you should use them in your bio and on every single post. Of course, you need to be sure they relate to your content, but the more the better! Maybe you know you need them, but you aren't sure which ones or why.

Hashtags on Instagram are far more than mere adornments to your captions—they are the bloodline that connects your content to a broader audience, acting as a potent tool to categorize, label, and increase the visibility of your posts to relevant users. They function as the signposts guiding Instagram's complex algorithm to suggest posts to users, making it easier for your potential followers to discover your content amid the deluge of images and videos populating their feed.

The secret sauce, however, lies not just in using hashtags, but in choosing the right ones. A finely curated selection of hashtags can resonate with your audience, mirror your brand identity, and even establish or consolidate your presence in a niche community.

One might be tempted to think that throwing in a larger number of hashtags could cast a wider net, drawing in more views. However, research indicates that Instagram's algorithm doesn't necessarily favor posts overflowing with hashtags. In fact, posts packed with too many hashtags could run the risk of being flagged as spam by the platform's algorithm, leading to decreased visibility or even potential penalization.

So what's the ideal approach to leverage the power of hashtags? Instead of indiscriminately stuffing your posts, focus on relevance and specificity. Look for hashtags that align with your content and are likely to be used by your target audience.

Understand the popularity and competitiveness of your chosen hashtags. While highly popular ones might expose your content to a larger audience, your post could also be quickly buried under newer posts. On the other hand, niche hashtags can keep your post visible for a longer duration and reach a more engaged audience.

In addition, consider using branded hashtags. These unique tags could enhance your brand identity, encourage user-generated content, and even enable you to track your engagement more effectively.

Remember, just like any other aspect of your social media strategy, an effective use of Instagram hashtags requires research, experimentation, and iterative refinement. Monitor your post performances, keep an eye on evolving trends, and don't be afraid to shake things up. After all, a flexible strategy is often the most rewarding one on the dynamic stage of social media.

Did you know there are five different types to consider?! Here's the rundown:

- **Location.** This would be your location and includes country, state, city, county, neighborhood, and specific places like the local stadium or concert.

- **Branded.** This would be anything related to your brand—events, campaigns, sales, etc.

- **Community.** Not to be confused with location, this is your group. It could be your quilting guild or hiking club, etc.

- **Descriptive.** It is exactly like what it sounds. A description of what you post. Dinner at Hideaway or Christmas lights at the capitol.

- **Industry.** Last but not least, you have industry-related posts and hashtags. If you are a nurse, vet, or real estate broker, your hashtags will relate to that industry.

Remember the original intent. Build community! Share interests and make meaningful connections. Use the hashtags to target the algorithm and reach the right people.

LinkedIn Strategies

LinkedIn, once a simple online résumé and job posting platform, has evolved significantly over the years. Today, it serves as a dynamic community connecting industry professionals, fostering talent recruitment, and building robust business-to-business (B2B) relationships. With over 700 million active users worldwide, LinkedIn is more relevant and vibrant than ever, especially for business owners, freelancers, and employees looking to broaden their professional network.

However, amid the platform's growing popularity, the challenge lies in differentiating yourself or your business from the crowd. To truly shine on LinkedIn, a unique and engaging approach is vital.

Let me illustrate with a real-life success story: One of my clients, a budding tech start-up, effectively leveraged LinkedIn to grow its network and industry visibility. Its strategy was a fine blend of content variety, personal interaction, and the leverage of trending industry topics.

First, the client maintained a diverse mix of posts, alternating between company updates, industry news, insightful blog posts, and even team spotlight features, which lent a more human face to the company. By providing a range of content, the company was able to engage different segments of its audience, from potential clients and partners to prospective employees.

Next, it was diligent and sincere in its interactions. It responded to comments on its posts, actively participated in relevant discussions, and reached out to connect with industry professionals. This interaction not only helped to build relationships but also provided valuable insights into its audience's interests and concerns.

Finally, the company rode the wave of trending industry topics. When a significant tech event or breakthrough was making the rounds, the company ensured its voice was part of the conversation, sharing insights or thoughtful commentary on its posts.

The company's strategic approach significantly improved its LinkedIn presence. One of its posts, a thought-provoking piece on the future of AI technology, gained considerable traction, earning a high number of likes, shares, and comments. This not only boosted the company's visibility but also sparked meaningful conversations with industry influencers.

Indeed, LinkedIn's increasing popularity presents a fertile ground for growth and networking. However, the key to standing out lies in authentic engagement, thoughtful content, and active participation in the professional community.

To start, you need to know your audience! Insider tip—use LinkedIn's website demographics tool to see who is visiting your website. Once you know your audience, you can cater your content to its needs. Build that community's organic visibility. Engage and start conversations. Comment on posts. Join groups!

Yes, LinkedIn is geared toward business and professionalism. However, the platform is desperate for the human element, just like the others. This is a great place to prove you have a business culture in which others want to be involved. Users also want information—consider more educating and less entertaining. Short "Did you know" or "Have you heard" content with infographics works well. It's okay to have a little fun with it to stop the scroll, but keep it PG!

Need some quick-fire best practices for LinkedIn? Consider the following:

- **Be personable.** Promoting yourself usually doesn't do as well as showing your personality. Of course, self-promotion is necessary, but keep it to a minimum.

- **PARTICIPATE.** Make sure you are engaged. Reply to comments, ask questions, and offer encouragement across all platforms.

- **Enhance readability.** Bullet points or a short paragraph with images is best. Have a Read More button to boost engagement with the information.

- **Add value.** Offer a challenge, opportunity, or benefit. When you provide something of value without self-promotion, you do two things—build credibility and build community.

- **Be consistent.** I will say it until I am blue in the face—it is that important. You can't pop in every other month or when you are looking for something. You need to be immediately recognizable and not the one that someone has to work to remember who you are or what you do.

X Strategies

X's real-time nature and character limits set it apart from other social media platforms, but many principles—like the importance of following trends, maintaining consistency, and leveraging hashtags—still apply. Despite the platform's emphasis on instant communication, you can strategize and streamline your engagement to make it more manageable and effective.

An aspect that makes X unique is its "real-time" aspect. It's a place where news breaks and conversations flow freely, all in the blink of an eye. This immediacy requires a more responsive approach than what might work on platforms like Instagram or LinkedIn.

However, you don't have to be glued to your X feed 24/7 to make the most of this platform. With a bit of forethought and the right tools, you can manage the flow of communication more efficiently. For instance, X offers a feature that allows you to create canned responses for common questions or interactions, saving time without losing the personal touch.

In my own X/Twitter journey (@_katiebrinkley), I've found a blend of strategic planning and real-time engagement works best. For example, during a major industry event (like Social Media Marketing World and CEX), I scheduled tweets ahead of time to share my insights on key topics on the agenda. However, I also remained active during the event, responding to real-time developments and joining ongoing conversations. This approach allowed me to maintain a consistent presence while also engaging directly with my followers and the broader X community.

One particular tweet, sharing a provocative question about the future of social media marketing, hit home. It generated significant interaction, including retweets and an engaging conversation thread. The key to this tweet's success was a blend of careful timing, relevance to current trends, and a call to action that encouraged responses.

While X's real-time nature and character limits might require a slightly different strategy, the platform offers unique opportunities for engagement. By leveraging features like canned responses and balancing planned posts with real-time interaction, you can create a dynamic X presence that fosters lively conversations and a growing follower base.

One thing you need to keep in mind is that you have to be more creative and thoughtful with your post. You can't have 50 hashtags and ramble for an entire paragraph. Short and sweet is key! Also, X recommends two things when building your X content calendar. Its business website shares:

The Rule of Thirds

- One-third of your Tweets promote your business or drive conversions.

- One-third of your Tweets share curated content from industry thought leaders.

- One-third of your Tweets involve personal interaction with your followers.

The 80-20 Rule

- 80 percent of your Tweets are designed to inform, educate, or entertain.

- 20 percent of your Tweets directly promote your business or drive conversions.

X.com Business content calendar tip: "Holidays, sporting events, and cultural events are all regular opportunities for you to connect with your audience and reach new followers."

Last but not least, the newcomer to the block—TikTok!

TikTok Strategies

Don't breeze past this section—TikTok isn't just a platform for teenagers and budding influencers. It has rapidly emerged as a powerhouse of viral content that spans audiences of all ages and interests. While it may be infamous for its dance trends and comedic skits, TikTok is also an effective platform for branding, education, and business promotion.

The unique aspect of TikTok is its capacity to propagate trends rapidly. A catchy dance routine or a creative skit can spread like wildfire across the platform, quickly jumping into other social media platforms like Facebook or X. It's not uncommon for TikTok content to lead the trend curve, with other social media platforms playing catch-up. So don't be surprised if you see a TikTok video go viral on Facebook, only to have TikTok users comment, "Oh, we moved past that trend last week." This might seem exaggerated, but in the fast-paced world of TikTok, it's quite close to reality.

From a business perspective, it's about finding your niche and creating engaging, fun, or informative content that aligns with your brand. For example, I've been exploring TikTok as part of my social media strategy, sharing snippets of my work and insights into the world of social media marketing.

One particular TikTok video I created—a short, fun explainer about the importance of hashtag use on social media—generated a lot more engagement than I anticipated. It was quick, digestible, and practical, striking a chord with TikTok's dynamic user base.

I've worked with clients who've leveraged TikTok to great success. One such client was a lawyer who was having trouble reaching potential new clients. Together we devised a TikTok strategy to raise her profile in the community. She created videos showing what a typical day was like for her—meeting with clients, researching cases in the law library, preparing documents. The behind-the-scenes look at the day-to-day work of a lawyer resonated with viewers. The TikTok quickly went viral in our area, gaining over 100,000 views. Soon the lawyer was flooded with calls from local news outlets saying they saw her on TikTok and they'd like to have her insights on upcoming legal matters that were featured in the news. The influx of new business from the social media exposure was astonishing. It just goes to show how a simple yet engaging TikTok video can connect with an audience and dramatically impact a business or professional practice.

Remember, it's not about being a part of every trend or making the most viral content—it's about building a brand presence and engaging with your audience in a creative and authentic way. If you approach TikTok with this mindset, you'll find it to be a valuable addition to your social media toolkit.

Now you may ask why you would want to be on TikTok when Instagram basically does the same thing with Reels. First, I would say consider the demographics. Who is your target audience? If you target 25- to 34-year-olds, then Instagram is where you find them. However, half of TikTok users are in the 18-to-24 age group. So if you want to target Gen Z, you have to be on TikTok.

Another thing to consider is video length. Instagram is limited to 90 seconds. Whereas TikTok videos can go up to 10 minutes.

The "like" and "share" features are also worth mentioning. First, TikTok gives you the ability to create folders and save your favorite videos in categories. You could have a recipe folder, a books folder, or a side-hustle folder (Instagram has copied this folder and pinning feature). In this way, TikTok is almost like Pinterest. And speaking of pinning— you can pin videos to the top of your feed. Most platforms have this function now, including Instagram!

TikTok is all about the trends and challenges. So the best way to fit into the algorithms and get noticed is to watch what is trending, be creative, and hop on! Of course, some trends may not be business appropriate, but there is so much to choose from, and it changes all the time, that you might hit on something and go viral before you know it. The key is to create a video while you are in your element, so to speak. TikTok is the perfect platform to be authentic. For example, you may find a trending song or voiceover that works perfectly with your brand or style. With a little creativity, you could end up with thousands of views within a day. The best part—you can cross-post or share the video to other platforms.

As with the other platforms, keep in mind that you need to use related hashtags, preferably trending or community-related. You also want to engage with comments and influencers on the platform. And— you guessed it—be consistent!

———————

Chapter 7

Podcasts and YouTube

Podcasts and YouTube hold unique positions within the digital marketing landscape. While not traditional social media platforms, they are pivotal channels in many successful marketing and social media strategies. Due to their distinctive roles and impacts, I've decided to spotlight them in a separate category, shining a light on their individual strengths and the ways they can enhance your overall marketing strategy.

Podcasts and YouTube, despite their differences, share a common ground as engaging, content-rich mediums. They offer a platform for in-depth exploration of topics, personal storytelling, and direct audience connection, making them highly effective tools in establishing and growing your digital presence. As we delve into their specific traits, similarities, and differences, we'll discuss practical strategies for integrating them into your marketing and social media plans.

So let's journey into the world of podcasts and YouTube, exploring the immense potential they hold for enriching your marketing strategy and amplifying your brand presence.

What Are Podcasts?

Podcasts are a modern reincarnation of the classic radio show format, with a significant twist: the power of on-demand consumption. They are digital audio recordings that cover an extensive range of topics. From entertainment and education to news and storytelling, podcasts deliver content in an accessible and convenient format.

While some podcasts are stand-alone episodes, most are part of a larger series where each installment builds on or complements the others. This episodic nature allows creators to delve deeper into their chosen subject matter, while listeners can subscribe and follow along as new content is released.

One of the defining attributes of podcasts is their flexibility. Unlike live radio or television, podcasts can be enjoyed whenever it suits the listener's schedule, whether that's during a commute, at the gym, or as a part of an evening wind-down routine. This convenience factor is a key reason for the growing popularity of the medium.

Podcasts can be accessed and enjoyed on various devices. Computers and smartphones are the most common, with apps like Apple Podcasts, Spotify, and Google Podcasts making it easy to subscribe and listen. Moreover, with the increasing prevalence of smart speaker devices like Amazon Echo and Google Home, you can also tune in to your favorite podcast while cooking dinner, cleaning, or even taking a shower!

In essence, podcasts blend the in-depth exploration of a book, the episodic nature of a TV show, and the convenience of a music playlist into a single package. They are a unique tool for learning, entertainment, and connection with a global community.

The History of Podcasts

Podcasts, while a quintessentially modern phenomenon, have their roots deep within the history of broadcast media, particularly radio. The advent of podcasting, as we know it today, can be traced back to the early 2000s when the technology to create digital audio files and disseminate them over the internet was becoming readily accessible.

The term 'podcast' combines 'iPod,' Apple's once-dominant portable media player, and 'broadcast' to create a new form of digital media. While British journalist Ben Hammersley mentioned the term in a 2004 article for The Guardian, thereby popularizing it, it's technology enthusiasts like Adam Curry who are often credited for bringing the podcasting concept into mainstream awareness. Adam Curry's show, 'Daily Source Code,' was instrumental in setting the stage for the format's broader acceptance.

The first recognized instance of a podcast was an episode of the public radio show This American Life that was made available for download in 2004. Its success sparked a revolution. The podcasting platform allowed for a democratization of broadcasting, making it accessible to anyone with a recording device, internet connection, and something to say. The low cost of entry meant that people were not just consumers of content but could also become creators.

Since that initial entry, podcasting has seen an exponential growth in popularity. What began as a niche medium for tech enthusiasts has grown into a mainstream medium with an ever-growing roster of shows spanning an incredible range of topics. From educational programming to true crime stories, self-help advice to political commentary, comedy shows to celebrity interviews—there's a podcast out there for virtually every interest.

In the past decade, podcasting has seen significant development, becoming a multi-billion-dollar industry with millions of episodes available across various platforms. Podcasts have also adapted to evolving technology, with many incorporating video, live-streaming, and interactive elements.

Despite the rapid evolution and increased commercialization, the heart of podcasting remains the same: it's a medium that offers a unique and personal way for people to share and receive stories, ideas, and information. With the continuing development of digital technology and the growing demand for on-demand content, the future of podcasting looks incredibly bright.

What Is YouTube?

Launched in 2005, YouTube is a video-sharing platform that has transformed the landscape of digital media. YouTube's premise is simple: it allows users to upload, share, view, rate, and comment on videos. What sets it apart from traditional broadcast media like television, though, is its user-generated and interactive nature. YouTube empowers individuals to become creators and curators of content, rather than merely consumers.

However, the scope of YouTube extends far beyond its basic function as a video-sharing website. In terms of sheer volume, YouTube is the second-largest search engine in the world, coming in after its parent company, Google. The platform has an immense and diverse range of content, from user-generated videos to professionally produced series, catering to virtually every interest, hobby, or educational need. YouTube videos encompass an incredibly broad spectrum—from vlogs (video blogs), how-to tutorials, and product reviews to music videos, full-length films, TV shows, and even live streams of events happening across the globe.

YouTube also serves as a social platform, fostering communities around specific niches or interests. Users can interact with creators and fellow viewers through comments, likes, and shares and even create their own playlists of preferred content. For many users, YouTube is also a source of income, with popular creators earning revenue through ads, sponsorship deals, and the platform's partnership program.

YouTube has been influential in shaping internet culture and trends. Viral YouTube videos often cross over into mainstream media and have a significant impact on popular culture. It's also become a launchpad for many talents, with several artists, comedians, and influencers getting their start on YouTube before transitioning to more traditional forms of media.

In short, YouTube is more than just a video-sharing website. It's a multifaceted platform for content creation, discovery, and consumption; a community builder; a cultural trendsetter; and a significant player in the global media ecosystem.

The History of YouTube

As stated earlier, YouTube launched in 2005. The company was started by three former PayPal employees, Chad Hurley, Steve Chen, and Jawed Karim, who decided to create a platform where users could upload and share videos easily. The motivation behind this groundbreaking idea is attributed to a couple of key events—the difficulty in sharing videos taken at a dinner party and the inability to find online clips of significant current events, like the 2004 Indian Ocean tsunami and Janet Jackson's infamous "wardrobe malfunction" at the Super Bowl.

In February 2005, the trio registered the domain name "YouTube. com," and by April 23rd, the first video, titled Me at the Zoo and featuring cofounder Jawed Karim, was uploaded. This marked the birth of a platform that would dramatically change the internet landscape. Despite its humble beginnings, YouTube's growth was explosive. By July 2005, people were uploading 8,000 videos a day; and by November, that number had skyrocketed to 25,000.

This rapid ascent did not go unnoticed. In November 2006, less than two years after its creation, YouTube was purchased by Google for a staggering $1.65 billion in stock, signaling its monumental value and potential influence in the world of online media. The Google acquisition gave YouTube the necessary infrastructure and resources to scale further, evolving into the behemoth it is today.

YouTube's rise was not entirely smooth, with challenges including copyright issues and controversial content. Yet these hurdles have not impeded its growth. Today, YouTube stands as one of the internet's most dominant forces, boasting over 2 billion logged-in users monthly, with more than a billion hours of video watched daily. From the platform's ability to catapult individuals to stardom overnight to its role as a global stage for sociopolitical discourse, YouTube has undeniably changed how we create, consume, and interact with video content in the digital age.

The Similarities Between Podcasts and YouTube

There are quite a few similarities between podcasts and YouTube videos. For one thing, they're both easily consumable content that you can enjoy without putting in a lot of effort. You can listen to a podcast while you're doing the dishes or working out, and you can watch a YouTube video while you're on the bus or taking a break at work.

They're also both great ways to learn new things. There are podcasts about history, science, true crime, and just about any other topic you can think of. And on YouTube, you can find videos about how to do just about anything. Finally, they're both great platforms for entertainment.

Both YouTube and podcasting have social media-like features. For example, you can like, share, and comment on either. However, the content will not show up on a news feed-type platform based on algorithms. Interaction becomes dependent on people going directly to your channel, site, or link. In this way, it is more of a closed circuit.

The Differences Between Podcasts and YouTube

Podcasts and YouTube each offer unique advantages depending on the nature of the content and the preferences of the audience. As a starting point, the most obvious difference between the two is their mode of delivery: YouTube is a visual platform, offering both audio and visual content, while podcasts are audio-only.

The visual element of YouTube can be critical for content where seeing is essential to comprehension, such as tutorials or how-to guides. Podcasts, on the other hand, offer a different kind of flexibility, allowing listeners to engage with content while performing other tasks that may preclude the use of visual media, such as driving, exercising, or even working.

The duration and engagement levels of content also differ significantly between the two platforms. YouTube videos tend to be shorter, providing quick bursts of entertainment or information, perfect for an audience with limited attention spans or time constraints. Podcasts, conversely, cater to long-form content, with most episodes lasting at least 15 to 20 minutes, and some even extending beyond an hour.

The longer format of podcasts is not a deterrent to their audience. On the contrary, recent studies have shown impressive engagement rates. According to a 2020 survey by the podcast hosting platform Podtrac, 74 percent of podcast listeners usually finish the episodes they start. An analysis by Podnews in the same year revealed an average completion rate around 80 percent, and a 2018 study by Acast noted that an average of 60 percent of listeners finish entire episodes. Remarkably, recent reports indicate that approximately 84 percent of podcast listeners now complete the whole episode, a statistic that underlines the engaged, dedicated nature of podcast audiences.

The content created for YouTube or a podcast can serve multiple purposes, especially in a digital era keen on content repurposing. The visually appealing content from YouTube videos can be creatively turned into Instagram Stories or Pinterest posts. Similarly, insightful excerpts from podcast interviews can be used as tweet threads or LinkedIn posts, demonstrating the utility and versatility of these platforms in reaching and engaging with audiences in diverse ways.

These distinctions illustrate that podcasts and YouTube cater to different audience needs and consumption patterns. Whether one platform is superior to the other is subjective and depends entirely on the content you aim to share and the preferences of your target audience.

Incorporating Podcasts and YouTube into Your Marketing Strategy

Knowing that a podcast or YouTube video will be longer than a social media post, you can employ your marketing strategy as a funnel. Your Facebook, Instagram, LinkedIn, and other accounts are the vehicles to transport followers to your website, YouTube channel, and podcast. Here are a few ideas on how you can use YouTube and podcasts to enhance your presence and build a community:

- Use podcasts to show off your knowledge about your industry. If you're an expert in your field, start a podcast and use it to share your knowledge with the world. You can even use it for interviewing other experts in your industry and getting their insights.

- Use YouTube videos to show off your products or services. If you have a physical product, create a video that shows it being used. If you have a service, create a video that explains what it is and how it works.

- Use both podcasts and YouTube videos to drive traffic to your website or blog. Include links to your website or blog in the description of your podcast episodes and YouTube videos, and make sure to mention them at the beginning and end of each one.

- Use both platforms to build relationships with potential and current customers. Respond to comments on your YouTube videos and engage with people who leave reviews for your podcast episodes. This will help you build rapport and trust with your audience.

- Use both platforms to create an overall brand for your business. Make sure that your podcast episodes and YouTube videos have a consistent look and feel, and that they reflect the overall branding of your business. This will help you build recognition and credibility for your brand.

Throughout my career in digital marketing, I've found that podcasts and YouTube serve as invaluable resources in any marketing strategy. They aren't just additional channels—they're vital tools for connection, promotion, and community building.

I took the plunge into podcasting in 2020, transitioning my background in radio into a new, digital medium. Admittedly, I was initially unsure of the content I could produce weekly without sounding repetitive, but once I began, my confidence soared along with my opportunities. My podcast evolved into a powerful tool for generating leads, networking, and establishing myself as a thought leader. These are facets of engagement and business growth that can't be replicated in a simple social media post.

Then I ventured into YouTube. I started recording my podcast episodes via Riverside and repurposing the video content for YouTube, effectively granting myself access to an entirely new audience. This process of repurposing content allowed me to extend my reach far beyond my podcast, infiltrating new digital spaces with valuable insights. As of now, while most of my downloads still occur via the podcast, my

YouTube channel's growth is gaining momentum every day.

In my experience, running a podcast or YouTube channel is akin to possessing a treasure trove of content. Each episode or video can be repurposed and reshaped into multiple social media posts, diversifying your digital presence. A single podcast episode could birth several quotable snippets for X, inspire an insightful blog post, or be transformed into an engaging carousel for Instagram. The possibilities are endless.

My journey with podcasts and YouTube reaffirms their critical roles in a comprehensive marketing strategy. They're more than just platforms—they're robust tools enabling you to amplify your reach, engagement, and influence in the digital sphere.

Chapter 8

————

The Four-Post Strategy

As we've explored in previous chapters, social media often feels like a necessary evil for modern businesses. Platforms constantly push us to post more content, share more updates, and be more active—all in the name of reach and engagement.

"Post more!" they urge. "Be more active!" they insist. But what many social media gurus neglect to mention is that excessive posting can actually backfire. Creating content just for the sake of keeping your feed populated leads to fatigue—for both you and your audience.

When every day is an endless scramble to churn out posts and videos, you end up drained. And your followers become numb to the barrage of content vying for their attention. Social media starts to feel like a loud, crowded marketplace rather than a means for meaningful connection.

But what if I told you there was a better way? A way to achieve real results, build your community, and generate leads while actually posting less content. A way to regain sanity amid the social media frenzy.

I'm excited to unveil a strategy that I've seen generate substantial growth for businesses while reducing their workload—the four-post strategy. This proven formula leverages the awareness-to-action continuum to maximize the impact of your content. By blending informative, helpful, promotional, and community-focused posts, you can increase engagement and conversions efficiently. Less becomes more with this cadence.

The four-post strategy works seamlessly across platforms, providing a consistent content framework tailored to how people actually consume information online. Whether you're on Facebook, Instagram, LinkedIn, or X, the awareness-to-action flow adapts beautifully.

This approach aligns perfectly with the original intention behind social media—to foster connections, not just bombard people with sales pitches. The four-post method enables you to engage more authentically by spacing out promotional content between value-adding posts.

As we delve into the framework, you'll learn:

- How to hook attention with digestible "awareness-stage" content

- Tips for delivering value through targeted educational posts

- The importance of humanizing your brand with behind-the-scenes community content

- When and how to effectively incorporate calls to action

- Real-world examples of the four-post strategy in action across platforms

By the end of this chapter, you'll have a proven blueprint for achieving your social media goals while keeping your sanity intact. No more aimless posting or content fatigue. Just an optimized road map for results. Let's start unpacking this transformative approach, beginning with the first pillar . . .

The Awareness Post

This post hooks attention with digestible information—think bright graphics, eye-catching stats, or quick video explainers. On Instagram, this is your Reels or a polished image post. On LinkedIn, consider a poll. These posts cast a wide net, attracting viewers through an intriguing teaser of what's to come.

The awareness stage is all about piquing interest with creative, snackable content. You want to capture attention amid busy feeds using succinct but effective posts tailored to each platform. Give people just enough of a preview to leave them wanting more.

For example, an awareness post on Instagram might be:

- A stylish graphic with an intriguing statistic (e.g., "58 percent of shoppers will abandon their cart. Don't let sales slip away!")

- A short Reel how-to or listicle video (e.g., "The top three tricks for reducing shopping cart abandonment")

- An eye-catching image relying on visual storytelling (e.g., a photo of a spilled bag of flour captioned "Don't let the details get messy")

The goal is to hook your audience's interest using whatever creative tactics fit best with your brand. Keep the content succinct, optimizing it for short attention spans. Ask a thought-provoking question; share an unexpected stat; provide a digestible how-to preview—give followers just enough to entice them to stick around for more.

On LinkedIn, your awareness post might take the form of:

- A quick poll asking about people's experiences with your topic

- A status update that can highlight something unexpected— maybe a provocative stance, surprising number, or conversation-starting assertion

- A discussion-prompting video under 60 seconds long

On LinkedIn, an effective awareness post grabs attention by revealing unexpected insights, data points, or perspectives aligned to your industry. Craft content that piques curiosity through informative infographics, intriguing statistics, interactive polls and more. Ensure it reflects your brand voice and areas of expertise.

On Facebook, an effective awareness post serves to pique curiosity and interest among your audience. Here are some ideas:

- A single sentence saying a statement or unpopular opinion to drive conversation using a Facebook template with a colorful background.

- A Reel that is 30 seconds or less with listicle-type information.

The goal is to capture attention and stir curiosity with novel, unexpected, visually impactful or interactive content. Tailor your awareness post format to align with your brand voice and industry.

Tailor your awareness content to each platform's unique style while keeping the core focus the same—generate intrigue and pique people's curiosity. You're casting a wide net here, capturing as many eyes as possible with the teaser.

The Tip/Tutorial Post

You've piqued people's interest—now deliver value by going a layer deeper. Provide a practical tip or a step-by-step tutorial expanding on your initial post. Turn that awareness-phase graphic into a carousel or video walking through actionable advice. Lead your audience from curiosity to capability with this engaging next installment.

For instance, if your opening Instagram Reel offered "Five Quick Hacks for Reducing Shopping Cart Abandonment," your subsequent post could elaborate on one or two of those hacks in detail. Educate your followers on specific tactics they can implement right away.

On Facebook, an effective follow-up to your attention-grabbing brand awareness graphic might be an educational video breaking down action steps to actually put those ideas into practice.

The key is increasing the value with each installment. Give people enough context to walk away understanding concrete concepts, not just high-level ideas. Enable your audience to progress from curiosity to capability.

Some examples of excellent tip/tutorial posts:

- An Instagram carousel outlining a step-by-step recipe after an appetizing awareness post

- A LinkedIn article elaborating on key skills after an intriguing poll result

- A Facebook video demonstrating EMDR therapy techniques after an informative statistic

- A tweet thread expanding on productivity tips initially shared in an engaging image post

The educational focus sets the tone here. Avoid overt selling; simply share your expertise. Craft your content for different learning styles—combine visuals, text, polls, and videos to convey the tips clearly.

The Community Post

Next in the four-post sequence comes the crucial community-building content. Here your goal shifts from teaching to relating. Humanize your brand and connect with the people in your audience by giving them a glimpse behind the curtain.

For example, an interior designer could follow up her tip posts with an Instagram Story showing her curating samples at a fabric shop. No educational element or direct selling—just a peek into her creative process.

Quote a testimonial from a satisfied client; recognize an employee; share a company milestone—the focus is on fostering relationships, not conversions. Strengthen your know-like-trust factor before moving into the final action post.

On LinkedIn, excellent community content might include:

- Introducing a new team member

- Behind-the-scenes photos/video from an event

- Sharing a story of how your business has used a product or service and how it impacted your business

- Sharing a customer review or testimonial

Think authenticity, transparency, and celebration of common interests. The community stage sets you up for a natural transition into your call to action while avoiding a solely sales-focused tone.

The Action Post

Finally, we've arrived at the action stage of the four-post journey. Here you incorporate an explicit call to action to convert the interest and goodwill built up from the previous posts.

The action post should offer something clearly valuable tied to your earlier content—a free consultation, discounted offer, lead magnet, etc. But be strategic about your CTA rather than blurting out a sales pitch.

For example, a fitness coach could conclude his four-post Instagram content batch with:

- A link in his bio to sign up for a 50 percent-off coaching assessment

- A coupon code for 30 percent-off supplements after his tutorial posts

- A prompt to book a free intro coaching call

The key is making the CTA feel like a natural next step versus an abrupt sales push. After nurturing your followers with awareness, education, and community-building content, they'll be primed to take action.

On X, excellent action post options include:

- A final tweet in a thread with a link to download your e-book

- A promotional tweet targeting followers of your handle with a limited-time coupon

- A summary tweet linking to your latest blog post with an opt-in giveaway

- A call for submissions to an upcoming virtual event or webinar

Experiment with different offers and formats to determine what resonates best with your audience on each platform. Track conversions to optimize your action-stage posts over time.

And remember—restraint and relevance are key. Avoid plastering sales messages in every post. Strategically incorporate CTAs only after first establishing value and authority. This earns you the right to guide your audience gently toward action.

In our distraction-filled online world, a considered, less-is-more approach to social media will drive results while retaining engagement. The four-post blueprint guides you there, moving purposefully from connection to conversion.

Goals and Principles of the Four-Post Strategy

Implementing the four-post blueprint on your social platforms has multiple advantages:

- **It reduces the pressure for constant content creation.** Rather than scrambling to populate your feed daily, you can thoughtfully craft your content in manageable batches. Less burnout, more sustainability.

- **It crafts cohesive mini-storylines.** Each four-post batch connects to tell a broader narrative that engages your audience. Education and entertainment, not just promotion.

- **It balances community and promotion.** Spacing out CTAs retains engagement rather than becoming overly salesy. Followers first, customers second.

- **It adapts across platforms.** Tailor post types and formats to each platform while retaining the logical four-stage flow. Optimize; don't homogenize.

To make the most of the four-post strategy, keep these core principles in mind:

- **Align with audience needs.** Understand your followers' interests to create relevant, valuable content that resonates. Research is key.

- **Maintain consistent branding.** Stay on brand with messaging and visual identity across posts to boost recognition. Cohesion builds authority.

- **Increase value with each installment.** Moving from surface to depth, guide your audience along an educational journey with each post.

- **Time CTAs appropriately.** Place calls to action strategically within the four-stage flow for better conversion rates. Patience pays off.

While you can adapt the posting cadence to suit your own goals, the underlying methodology remains solid. In our distraction-filled online era, less can indeed be more. Avoid posting for posting's sake. Instead, implement the four-post blueprint to maximize your impact.

Now you have a proven formula to guide your content creation. Imagine finally gaining back time spent on social media while actually growing your brand. The four-post strategy makes it possible, moving seamlessly from connection to conversion.

The Four-Post Strategy in Action

Now that we've explored the core concepts, let's examine how real businesses can effectively apply this approach on key social platforms.

On Instagram

Sara founded a boutique wall art and home decor shop and leverages Instagram to promote her products. Here's how Sara can harness the four-post strategy:

- **Awareness.** A Reel or short-form video showcasing how Sara creates her art.

- **Tip.** A Reel tutorial showing how to stage a room using Sara's methods or wall art as a centerpiece.

- **Community.** A behind-the-scenes Story showing Sara at a local art fair, scouting pieces from emerging artists to potentially feature. Offers an authentic peek into her curation process.

- **Action.** A shoppable post showcasing new hand-painted vases available on her site, encouraging followers to browse the collection and purchase.

On Facebook

Steve is a financial advisor who aims to connect with potential clients on Facebook. Here's how:

- **Awareness.** An engaging graphic titled "How Much Does the Average American Spend on Impulse Purchases?" uses statistics to reveal surprising facts.

- **Tip.** In a one-minute video, Steve explains easy strategies that viewers can implement to curb impulsive spending and save more effectively. Offers helpful guidance.

- **Community.** Steve makes a post introducing his team, with photos, backgrounds, and fun facts about each member. Allows his audience to get to know the people behind his business.

- **Action.** A carousel ad for Steve's intro financial checkup service to create personalized money-saving plans, driving conversions.

On LinkedIn

Priya is a content marketing strategist who utilizes LinkedIn to establish herself as an industry leader. Her strategy:

- **Awareness.** Priya creates a LinkedIn poll asking her viewers a question about how much time they are spending on social media each week.

- **Tip.** She shares a LinkedIn article highlighting three ways that brands can repurpose blog posts on social media. Provides tactical value.

- **Community.** Priya congratulates a client on successful content marketing results since working together. Emphasizes how much time the client has gotten back since signing up to work with Priya. Social proof of expertise.

- **Action.** She advertises her different content marketing consulting packages to generate leads.

The four-post strategy can work for any brand on key platforms. Tailor the content while retaining the logical flow from awareness to action over each series of posts.

Track Success with Metrics

To optimize your four-post strategy over time, be sure to carefully track key metrics with each content batch. Consistently analyzing performance data will reveal what's working and what's falling flat. You'll gain insights to help refine your approach for maximum impact.

Here are some of the core metrics to monitor:

Awareness Engagement

- Analyze shares, comments, followers gained, and overall reach on your initial awareness-building posts. This gauges whether your teasers and graphics are grabbing attention as intended.

- Low engagement signals an awareness that content needs improvement. Brainstorm fresh formats and topics that align with audience interests.

- Compare engagement on awareness posts across platforms—is visual content performing better on Instagram versus LinkedIn? Tailor accordingly.

Traffic

- Measure website visits, email list sign-ups, and other clicks driven by your tip/tutorial and community posts. This reveals their impact at driving actions.

- Try adding UTMs to links to quantify exactly which platforms and posts deliver the most traffic.

- Unexpected results? Double down on the formats and topics sending higher traffic while switching up underperforming content.

Conversions

- Track email list growth, free consultation sign-ups, purchases, and other goals from your action posts. This indicates real ROI.

- Look for patterns—does a specific CTA or offer convert better than others? Test different calls to action and incentives to determine what motivates your audience.

- Low conversion rates signal misaligned offers or poor timing. Try revisiting action posts after adding more valuable content or with different promotional hooks.

Overall Reach

- Analyze total impressions and engagement for each full four-post batch. Look for overarching trends in topics, formats, and platforms resonating best with your audience.

- Consider your goals—are you prioritizing awareness, traffic, or conversions? Compare metrics with goals to ensure your content mix aligns.

Regularly monitoring performance data will reveal what's truly working and enable you to adapt your four-post strategy for maximum impact. The analytics will guide you, but only if you take the time to listen to what they're telling you.

By carefully implementing and tracking results of the four-post blueprint, you'll gain an optimized framework custom-tailored to your audience and goals. The path to social media success lies in the data.

In this chapter, we explored a strategy that provides clarity amid the social media clutter—the four-post approach. This proven formula gives you a content blueprint tailored to how people actually consume information online.

The awareness-to-action structure moves your audience smoothly through the conversion funnel. No more aimless posting or content fatigue. Just an optimized road map designed to engage and convert.

By implementing the four-post strategy, you gain:

- A sustainable content cadence that reduces burnout

- Cohesive mini-storylines crafted to captivate your audience

- A natural balance of community content and promotion

- Flexibility to customize posts across different platforms

Keep these core principles in mind as you plan and refine your four-post batches:

- Ensure content aligns with your audience's interests

- Maintain consistent messaging and branding

- Increase educational value with each installment

- Time calls to action appropriately to avoid a salesy tone

Be diligent in tracking key metrics like reach, traffic, and conversions. The data will reveal what's resonating so you can further optimize the framework.

In our distraction-laden digital era, less can truly be more when it comes to strategic content. Avoid posting just for posting's sake. Instead, embrace the four-post blueprint to maximize your impact while maintaining sanity.

Clarity, consistency, and community lie at the heart of social media success. This chapter provided the blueprint to get you there. Now venture forth and connect authentically with your audience—four posts at a time in the world of Web3 and the metaverse.

Chapter 9

Back to Community with Web3 and the Metaverse

Sometimes the way forward involves circling back to the basics. Social media at its core is about forging connections, sharing enriching memories and experiences, and fostering authentic interactions. It is in this essence where the future of social media—Web3 and the metaverse—truly shines, exploring fresh avenues for communication through unique offerings such as VIP memberships, group meetups, and immersive live 3D opportunities.

The evolution of social media, however, isn't without its ebbs and flows. Consider the case of non-fungible tokens (NFTs). Once a booming facet of the digital world, the popularity of NFTs has waned in 2023. High entry costs and unclear use cases have led many to deem NFTs as an extravagant fad past its prime. Yet it's important to remember that it's still early days for this technology.

While the NFT market experiences fluctuations, the core concept of using blockchain technology to create unique, verifiable digital assets is a powerful one. This underpinning idea holds the potential to revolutionize the way we engage with digital content. Already, we can see promising use cases for NFTs: they can represent ownership of digital artworks, enable the sale of digital tickets, prove the authenticity of digital collectibles, and gamify the ownership of digital assets.

Even if the name "NFT" fades into obscurity, the technology and its potential are likely to persist, evolving and taking new forms. The digital landscape is continually shifting, and those who can adapt to these changes and harness the power of authentic human connection through platforms like Web3 and the metaverse will stand miles ahead in the social media game. As we journey into this "new world," keeping our roots in community and personal connection will be paramount for success.

The Web3 Experience

Web3 is the next generation of the internet based on decentralized technologies. As mentioned previously, it will allow for more personalization and control over data, as well as increased security. This means that your audience or consumers can customize their experiences on the web. Think about it like this—when you go to the salon as a new client, the stylist will ask a bunch of questions to figure out what you want to do with your hair and whether it is realistic to achieve what you want. It takes time, and it may or may not turn out as you expected. However, if you have a relationship with a good stylist, he or she has taken detailed notes on what you like and what you don't like, what products work best on your hair, when you last visited—even notes on what you talked about before, during, or after the appointment.

Web 2.0 is the first experience, running through all the questions time after time—explaining what you want. Web3 is the second experience—what you like, what works, your history, and conversations at the ready, so you can jump in and have a relaxing experience without having to run through all the questions and details again and again.

The metaverse is a project that is working to create a 3D virtual world that will be built on top of Web3 technologies. So Web3 will be where your preferences and details are stored (like your handbag, wallet, cell phone, etc.), and the metaverse will be the world in which you shop and live. You will wander through and experience the metaverse by using Web3. Then when you find something in the metaverse that you want to join or purchase (an event, a community, a group, or even a team), you will use an NFT for access.

What Are NFTs?

NFTs can represent a diverse range of items from digital art to in-game items, and they can even serve as proof of purchase and ownership. Stored on a blockchain, NFTs can be bought, sold, or traded, functioning like currency or cryptocurrency, yet bearing a resemblance to trading cards or receipts. Their unique nature, unreplicable and distinct, makes them perfect for collectibles or bespoke experiences.

Despite the flux in NFT popularity, the tokens hold value in two significant ways: One is their potential as an investment tool, similar to unique artwork sold and resold over time, appreciating in value with each transaction. The other, perhaps less highlighted but equally meaningful, is their capacity to enhance experiences and foster community building.

In the metaverse, NFTs can symbolize a VIP membership, providing access to exclusive events, content, and experiences. Imagine securing a VIP concert ticket or a professional sporting event pass, represented by an NFT. This NFT could provide access to a virtual group where you could engage with the band or sports team in 3D before or after the event. Businesses could create NFT groups for their loyal customers, and we're already witnessing the formation of groups around shared interests like gaming, cooking, or fitness.

My personal experience with an NFT sports group has been exciting. During the Stanley Cup finals, I joined a chat within the group rooting for the Colorado Avalanche, my home team. To my delight, after their victory, one of the team players joined our chat and interacted with us. A real-time, immersive interaction like that couldn't be replicated on traditional social media platforms like Facebook or X. It's these transformative experiences, these new depths of community engagement and connection, that NFTs, enhanced by 3D interactions, bring to the table in the metaverse.

Remember that while NFTs may seem to be in a downward trend right now, the inherent technology and its potential are still evolving. Whether we call them NFTs or something else, the function they perform will likely persist and continue to shape the future of digital engagement.

3D Experiences for Business

Live 3D experiences are exactly what they sound like: opportunities to experience things in a three-dimensional, virtual space. They can be anything from classes to conferences. Live 3D experiences give you a chance to participate in events that you might not be able to attend in person.

Consider the number of times you wanted to participate in a meetup, class, or conference, but geographical boundaries held you back. The advent of NFTs and 3D experiences can break down these barriers, enabling you to host and attend events you'd never have thought possible. Platforms like Zoom have made virtual participation a reality, but they often fail to capture the true essence of such gatherings—the opportunity to network and CONNECT. This is where the metaverse shines.

Let's consider a hypothetical situation. Perhaps you've always aspired to participate in the prestigious TechCrunch Disrupt, an annual tech conference held in San Francisco. Unfortunately, the distance, time, and cost have kept you away. But with NFTs and the metaverse, this dream could become a reality.

By purchasing an NFT ticket, you could access TechCrunch Disrupt in the metaverse. Instead of viewing sessions through a 2D livestream, you would have an immersive 3D experience. Your avatar could explore the virtual venue, interact with other attendees, visit vendor stalls showcasing cutting-edge products, and network with entrepreneurs from across the globe—all without leaving your home.

The metaverse opens up transformative possibilities. Major conferences and events could have digital twins, allowing remote participants to mimic an in-person experience. You could establish a global professional network and foster an expansive community unbound by physical limitations. Vendors could showcase products in imaginative 3D environments tailored to each item.

In this hypothetical scenario, the metaverse effectively teleports you to San Francisco for a digitally enhanced version of TechCrunch Disrupt. The immersive capabilities create new avenues for networking, product exploration and community building in an engaging virtual setting.

Imagine the possibilities. Perhaps you've watched a complicated cooking tutorial and wished you could have a private lesson. With an NFT, you could theoretically gain access to a private cooking class in the metaverse with a renowned chef, allowing you to perfect that recipe.

What if you've been longing for a vacation to Italy but are unsure about the destination? With NFTs and the metaverse, you could embark on live 3D tours of Rome and Sicily, offering a taste of both locales and helping you make an informed decision.

As AI capabilities continue to rapidly evolve, these technologies are reshaping businesses and social media engagement in profound ways. AI is powering tools from chatbots to content curation, enabling more convenient and personalized digital experiences. However, as AI permeates our day-to-day lives, maintaining authentic human connection becomes more crucial than ever.

Amidst these technological shifts, social media remains a space for businesses to build trust and community by showing up authentically. While AI may handle certain logistics behind the scenes, success still hinges on resonating as a real, approachable brand. Fostering true connections supersedes any wizardry AI enables. By keeping community and transparency at the core of your social media presence, you ensure technology serves to enhance, not replace, meaningful relationship

Ever dreamed of shopping on the famed Rodeo Drive, but a weekend trip to LA doesn't fit your schedule? An NFT could grant you access to a 3D shopping experience, letting you browse and shop at your leisure.

The question now is, how can you leverage NFTs, Web3, and the metaverse for your business to create superior experiences and build a thriving community?

Chapter 10

How to Be an Early Adopter

As we journey into the brave new world of Web3, NFTs, the metaverse, and artificial intelligence (AI), there's a whole universe of opportunities waiting to be explored. In this digital era, your business and social media strategies can take a revolutionary leap forward. However, it's crucial to remember that embracing these emerging technologies isn't a sprint, but a marathon. It's not about instant mastery, but gradual learning and adaptation.

While innovations like AI, machine learning, the metaverse, and NFTs may feel overwhelming, remember that it's not too late to become an early adopter. The landscape is continuously evolving, and many businesses are still in the exploratory stages, making now the perfect time to start engaging.

When it comes to AI specifically, consider starting small by implementing chatbots for customer service or using AI to refine social media content. As abilities improve, progressively explore more advanced applications. Approach AI with patience and an experimental mindset.

The trick lies in not attempting to implement everything all at once. Rather, focus on understanding the fundamental principles; then progressively explore the different possibilities. Familiarize yourself with the dynamics of these technologies and their potential impact on your business. Start small, experiment, and learn from each experience.

This measured approach gives you the flexibility to adapt as these technologies mature. Remember, every journey starts with a single step. Now is your chance to take that first step toward the future of business and social media engagement. Here are some ideas:

- Use a Web3 browser like Brave when you surf the internet or post on social media.

- Start collecting NFTs that represent things you are interested in or experiences you want to have. For example, I have an NFT for a VIP ticket to a conference that is held every year. I might not be able to attend every year in person, but I can still participate in the experience virtually and interact with other attendees from around the world.

- Follow metaverse projects on social media, and start learning about what they are doing and how it could impact your industry.

- Use a Web3 wallet like MetaMask or Phantom when you make online purchases. This will help support businesses using these new technologies.

- Experiment with AI tools like chatbots or content generators to enhance customer service and social media engagement. Start small and incrementally build expertise.

- Research AI marketing tools that could help refine ad targeting, content creation, and campaign analytics. Consider a basic AI tool as a low-risk starting point.

The key is to start small and become familiar with the possibilities of Web3, NFTs, the metaverse, and AI. As you get more comfortable, incorporate them into your business and social media strategy. By being an early adopter, you'll have a competitive advantage and be ready to capitalize on future opportunities.

Don't Listen to the Naysayers

When you start chatting with friends, family, or peers about new technology, you will inevitably run into what I call the "fear factor." People fear what they don't understand or when they lack vision. We have a history of naysayers when it comes to advancements and tech, from the steam engine train and automobile to the radio and internet. If you look back, it may seem funny now, but in the heat of the moment, naysayers can create doubt. The doubt is often due to what anthropologists, psychologists, and sociologists call "moral panic." Moral panic is the widespread and irrational fear of something threatening the values, well-being, or interests of the public. It is an unjustified panic over a social issue.

Moral Panic and Fear

Moral panic often follows invention. To keep everything in perspective, look at some of the predictions and fears of technology through the years:

The 1750s and the Train

In the Victorian Era, it was believed that trains "injured the brain" and caused "railway madness." There were frequent reports of men going insane on the trains, and their illness was caused by the motion of the train. Incidents were frequent enough that the railways put policies in place to manage the madmen if there were an incident. The news media documented and reported incidents for decades.

Another moral panic related to the railways came from the medical community cautioning women about traveling at high speeds and dislocating their uterus at high speeds—yes, you read that right. A physician writing in the New England Medical Gazette said:

"If a woman sets out for a sea voyage or a journey by rail the day before her menses should appear, she will be very apt to skip one period, and perhaps more. Or, if the flow comes, she may experience greater suffering than usual. If it be too scanty, or too profuse, she may be very ill. As an indirect consequence, she will be likely to suffer from some form of uterine flexion or dislocation."

The doctor included peer support by quoting a second doctor that stated, "a displacement of the uterus is just as much an absolute fact as the occurrence of a hernial protrusion."

The 1800s and Radio

From respected newspapers to scientists, there was little faith in the future of the radio when it came out. The Boston Post in 1865 said, "Well-informed people know it is impossible to transmit the voice over wires and that were it possible to do so, the thing would be of no practical value;" and the Scottish physicist Sir William Thomson said in 1897, "Radio has no future." Ha!

Similarly, the telephone seemed to bring out the naysayers and fearmongers. In 1876, President Hayes asked Bell, "That's an amazing invention, but who would ever want to use one of them?"

The 1900s and the Automobile

Women didn't fare much better with the automobile. Automobiles were considered "devil wagons" and thought to cause hysteria, weakness, and fainting in women. In addition, there were protests due to how loud and fast the machines were. Early automobiles scared the carriage horses and killed countless animals on the road (roadkill). Of course, the cries to end the automobile were suppressed by the speed, convenience, and mobility it provided.

1995 and the Internet

In 1995, the internet was fairly new, and the David Letterman

Show was fairly popular. Behind the scenes, the show scheduled Bill Gates as a guest. Gates came on stage, and the two men exchanged the usual pleasantries. Then Letterman asked Gates if he knew anything about the internet. Gates explained the web and how it would be the next big thing. Not convinced, Letterman mocked Gates about listening to a baseball game on the internet. Letterman said:

"But I can remember a couple of months ago, there was like a big breakthrough announcement, that on the internet or on some computer deal, they were going to broadcast a baseball game—You could listen to a baseball game on your computer—And I just thought to myself, does radio ring a bell?"

You can see the clip by searching "Bill Gates explains this 'internet' thing" on YouTube.

The Present

It is easy to look back at past predictions and moral panic and laugh a little. I mean how crazy is it to think that women would dislocate their uterus by riding in a train or car. But if you look at the present and current moral panics, you may have a better understanding. Without going too political, we have people that truly feared the COVID vaccine. Before that, we had the "satanic panic" of the 1980s where parents were scared their daycare was run by witches.

Jump to the hot topic of this chapter, as we have people that believe Web3 isn't safe—it is a fad and will fall to the wayside.

While I skipped past MANY other failed predictions and moral panics throughout the decades, I think you get the point. We will have those that carry negative thoughts, challenge what they don't understand, or refuse to embrace technology. That's okay! I only hope you aren't one of them!

The most significant difference between the naysayers, or negative

Nancys, and you will be YOUR mindset. They will stick to what they know in a fixed mindset. Not you—you will embrace a growth mindset! But what's the difference, and why does it really matter? I'm glad you asked!

Embrace the Growth Mindset

Let's delve into a transformative concept that's been the cornerstone of modern psychology and self-improvement—the fixed versus growth mindset. Introduced by Stanford University psychologist Carol Dweck in her influential book Mindset: The New Psychology of Success in 2006, this concept has had a profound impact on how we approach learning, development, and motivation.

In her extensive research, Dweck identified two primary mindsets that people embody—a fixed mindset and a growth mindset. These mindsets drastically shape our perspectives on abilities, intelligence, and characteristics, profoundly influencing our motivation, resilience, and overall success across various life domains such as education, work, and relationships.

Starting with the fixed mindset—it's characterized by the belief that one's abilities and knowledge are set in stone. Individuals with a fixed mindset perceive life as a series of win-or-lose propositions, where resources and opportunities are scarce. They may become easily threatened by others' success and resistant to change, preferring to stick to the status quo even when it's ineffective.

For instance, in business, a fixed mindset could manifest as resentment when a competitor wins a bid. Rather than looking for ways to improve their offerings, individuals with a fixed mindset might resort to damaging the competition's reputation. They view new ideas as threats to their expertise and authority and may resist learning or adapting to changes. Consequently, a fixed mindset can significantly limit personal and professional growth, as it stifles the capacity to learn and adapt.

Continuing to the growth mindset—it's a perspective that epitomizes flexibility and openness to learning. People with a growth mindset firmly believe in the potential to develop and improve their abilities and intelligence throughout their lifetime. They approach life as a rich canvas of learning opportunities, viewing resources and possibilities as abundant rather than scarce.

Those with a growth mindset embrace new ideas, are willing to take calculated risks, and learn from their missteps, making it a potent tool in business and personal life. Given a situation where a competitor wins a bid, they would respond constructively. Instead of reacting negatively or undermining the competitor, they might congratulate the competitor and the client, offering complementary services or products to add value. This proactive approach underscores a readiness to learn and adapt, fostering innovative ways to succeed.

Additionally, they are keen to expand their horizons, invest in their skills, and refine their strategies, demonstrating a tenacious commitment to lifelong learning and self-improvement. Hence a growth mindset fuels continual progress toward achieving goals, emphasizing that our potential is never static but ever-evolving.

Both mindsets have their unique influence on our actions and attitudes. Understanding the distinction between these two mindsets can be a powerful tool, aiding in developing a more open, flexible, and growth-oriented approach to life and business. As you venture into the realms of Web3, NFTs, and the metaverse, adopting a growth mindset will serve as a beacon, guiding you through the challenges and changes that lie ahead.

Be a Connector

To become an early adopter, you have to connect. You need support to learn and grow—but you also want to add value to those that help you. If you haven't read The Tipping Point by Malcolm Gladwell, I highly recommend it. He talks about social epidemics, the law of the few, and how we are dependent on three groups of people.

First, the law of the few is that basic 80/20 rule—the idea that 80 percent of the work is done by 20 percent of the participants. The 20 percent are made up of three distinct groups: connectors, mavens, and salespeople. Here's the breakdown:

Connectors. These are the people who are constantly introducing you to someone. They are the network of your network. They know everyone across social, professional, cultural, and economic circles. If you need a recommendation for a painter, school, doctor, spiritual guide, restaurant, wine, or babysitter—they instantly send you a vCard (virtual business card) or share a contact on their phone. Connectors are the ones who have a talent for knowing everyone, and not just by name. They have a vast network. In social circles, they are the ones that mingle, ask questions, show interest, and have a certain energy or exude confidence.

Mavens. These are the walking Wiki pages. They consume information and then share and trade their knowledge. These are the people you go to before doing a Google search. Have you ever noticed on a Facebook or Nextdoor page that there is one person who knows the answer to everything but isn't as social on the site? This person is your maven. Mavens are the ones that will tell you everything you need to know about fixing the washing machine or that spot on your arm.

Salespeople. These are your negotiators. They have a talent for persuasion and charm that allows them to convince others. Salespeople excel at reading people to identify their needs and motivations. They then leverage this understanding to make a personalized pitch highlighting how their product or service is the perfect solution. Salespeople thrive on the art of the deal — they enjoy negotiations and have an innate ability to guide conversations towards a desired outcome. Whether selling you a new car, closing a business contract, or getting you to try a sample at the mall, salespeople are the ones who can win you over with an engaging conversation and a compelling case. Their mix of likability, persistence, and influence is a potent combination that makes them masters of selling.

By embracing the qualities of connectors, mavens, and salespeople in both the Web3 and social media landscapes, you set yourself up for success in these rapidly evolving domains.

As a connector, make it your mission to weave a vibrant network that bridges both realms. Link people from different backgrounds, professions, and areas of interest. Foster relationships, introduce collaborators, and build a diverse community that shares a common interest in exploring these novel spaces.

Embody the maven by staying voraciously curious about the ongoing developments in both social media and Web3. Always seek to learn more, dive deeper, and then share what you've gleaned with your network. This reciprocal exchange of information will not only fortify your grasp of the subject matter but also position you as a go-to resource in your network.

Lastly, don the hat of the salesperson by mastering the art of persuasive communication. As you traverse the worlds of social media and Web3, you'll often find yourself in situations where you need to articulate your ideas and vision compellingly, be it to drive adoption of a new tool within your team or to negotiate collaborative ventures.

Remember, these are not rigid roles, but characteristics you can embrace to enhance your journey as an early adopter in both the Web3 and social media environments. Through cultivating connectivity, sustaining a passion for knowledge, and developing persuasive prowess, you're well equipped to navigate and flourish in these dynamic domains. And as you grow, you also contribute to the strength and diversity of the community around these cutting-edge developments. Your journey, after all, is part of a larger tapestry of interconnected journeys, all contributing to the exciting evolution of our digital world.

Stories of Communities

In the grand arena of social media, amid the plethora of individual profiles, pages, and posts, exists an often overlooked element that possesses immense power—social media communities. These are not just people sharing, liking, or following, but collective clusters of individuals united by common interests, causes, or passions. They are the beating hearts within the vast body of social media.

Think of them as virtual campfires where like-minded people gather to exchange stories, seek advice, share experiences, and support one another. These communities might take shape as Facebook groups, dedicated X threads, Instagram hashtags, or LinkedIn networking circles, but their essence remains the same: They are spaces of collaboration and connection, driven by shared interests and mutual support.

Communities have the ability to galvanize people, spur innovative thoughts, and foster deep relationships. When individuals unite under common goals or interests, the potential for growth is limitless. To illustrate this power, we're going to delve into three separate stories that showcase the immense value and profound impact that communities can have in various aspects of our lives.

Story One: Sue B.'s Journey

"I think community is the cornerstone of any business. When you bring together

like-minded entrepreneurs who support each other, cheer for each other, and connect deeply with each other, being in business has more meaning, purpose, and impact."

—Sue B. Zimmerman, the Instagram Expert

I've had the pleasure of getting to know Sue B., known as The Instagram Expert, through social media. She adeptly cultivates her community, fostering connectivity through Instagram DM conversations, a Facebook group, and Slack. She also skillfully takes the community offline by hosting regular meetups throughout the world. This focus on community building has allowed Sue to create a sustainable and meaningful business model.

In the digital age, Sue's effective use of social media to build a community around her brand illustrates how online platforms can accelerate connections when leveraged correctly. By creating relevant and engaging content specifically for her community, she has fostered deeper connections and ultimately achieved greater success in her business.

Story Two: Alex Sanfilippo's Realization

"When my podcasting software business started taking off, community members always asked me, 'What are you up to, Alex? Is there anything else in the works right now?' I realized I had a problem—I wasn't communicating in a way that let people into my life/business . . . I made the following commitment: 'Alex Sanfilippo only posts content worthy of going viral among my community (not the world) that gives them access to what I'm doing and how I'm serving.' Since that day, my organic social media posts have become one of the primary growth tools for my business and strengthener of the community. Social media is powerful if you use it the right way!"

—Alex Sanfilippo, cofounder of PodMatch

Alex's experience elucidates the importance of leveraging social media to connect with and build community. By utilizing social media strategically, Alex managed to build deeper connections with his audience and create a sense of transparency and trust, leading to greater business success.

This approach is a clear demonstration of how offering glimpses into one's life and business activities can create a sense of transparency, fostering trust and engagement within the community. Alex's experience is a reminder that effective use of social media goes beyond surface-level promotion and calls for a strategic approach aimed at fostering deeper connections.

Story Three: Jodi's Experience—the Value of Online Communities

"One of the very first business programs I invested in had an online Facebook group; they also put us into accountability groups of four to meet virtually. . . When I was looking to have a baby as a single woman at 40, my doctor suggested I check out an online community called 'Single Moms by Choice'. . . I have also made a few friends in the group, one of which lived in NY at the time while I was in CA. . . She eventually moved to CA and now we live 5 minutes from one another and have regular play dates."

—Jodi

Jodi's journey with online communities beautifully illustrates how such spaces can serve as invaluable sources of support and connection. Her experience with a business-focused Facebook group demonstrates the enduring power of these relationships, with connections evolving into business partnerships and even offline friendships.

What stands out to me in Jodi's story is the common thread of support and camaraderie that binds the group, creating a network of individuals cheering for each other's success.

Her story further emphasizes the value of such communities in personal contexts. The Single Moms by Choice group provided a platform for shared experiences and advice, proving instrumental during her fertility journey. It's interesting to note how the bonds forged in the virtual world transcended into real-world friendships, underscoring the meaningful connections that can form in these online communities.

Jodi's experiences serve as a testament to the power of online communities in providing valuable support and fostering deep connections, in both professional and personal settings. It's a clear reminder of the unique role such platforms play in today's digital age, providing a sense of belonging and connectedness during various phases of our lives.

Join Social Media Communities

One of the most powerful forces in the modern digital world is the formation of communities. It has the ability to galvanize people, spur innovative thoughts, and foster deep relationships. When individuals unite under common goals or interests, the potential for growth is limitless. To illustrate this power, we're going to delve into three separate stories that showcase the immense value and profound impact that communities can have in various aspects of our lives.

Communities have become especially pivotal for entrepreneurs, creators, and small business owners. They serve as an invaluable resource for knowledge, inspiration, and collaboration, as well as a fertile ground for reaching potential customers and partners.

Let's dive into the narrative of Samantha, a small business owner, who tapped into the power of these vibrant digital ecosystems to broaden her reach, connect with fellow entrepreneurs, and ultimately expand her online jewelry business.

Samantha was a small business owner who sold handmade jewelry through her online store. Although she had a loyal group of customers, she struggled to reach new audiences and grow her business. She felt isolated and disconnected from other business owners and was unsure of how to connect with potential customers and partners.

One day, Samantha decided to join a Facebook group for small-business owners in her industry. She was initially hesitant, as she wasn't sure if the group would be a good fit for her or if she would be able to contribute to the conversation. But she decided to take a chance and join.

To her surprise, Samantha found that the group was full of supportive, like-minded individuals who were eager to help one another succeed. She began to participate in discussions, share her own experiences and expertise, and offer advice and support to other group members. She also started to post updates about her business and share her products with the group.

Over time, Samantha found that her involvement in the Facebook group had a number of benefits for her business. She made valuable connections with other business owners and potential customers, and she received valuable feedback and support from the group. She also gained new insights and ideas that helped her to improve her business and reach new audiences.

Ultimately, Samantha's decision to join the Facebook group proved to be a powerful way to build her community and connections for her business. By participating in the group and sharing her expertise, she was able to make valuable connections that helped her to grow and succeed.

This is just an example of how a social media group can help you grow your business. If you focus on becoming a connector, you will naturally build a community—a following. Being a connector is the intent of social media. Now you may think you aren't a connector, that you don't know that many people, or that you don't know where to start. I say, start by joining communities! When my curiosity for podcasting peaked, I chose to join communities and network with other podcasters.

As a social media manager, I knew there were options. You have options too! You can join groups and communities on every platform and for almost every interest.

Here's how to get started in social media communities and become a valuable member as a connector:

1. Lurk before you leap. When joining a new group or community, it's important to first observe the culture and etiquette. See what kinds of posts are popular and what types of comments are getting the most engagement. This insight will give you a good idea of what is acceptable and what isn't.

2. Add value. When you're ready to start participating, ensure you're adding value to the conversation. Share your insights and expertise, ask questions, and be helpful. Always keep your comments positive or help find solutions. Here are a few tips on how to add value to a Facebook group without seeming salesy:

- **Focus on providing helpful, useful content.** Instead of constantly promoting your products or services, try to provide value to the group by sharing helpful information, resources, and insights that are relevant to the group's interests.

- **Engage with other members.** Take the time to engage with other members of the group by commenting on their posts, answering questions, and offering support and advice. This helps to build trust and rapport, and it makes it more natural for you to share information about your business when appropriate.

- **Be authentic and transparent.** Be genuine and authentic in your interactions with the group, and be transparent about your business and what you have to offer. This helps to build trust and credibility, and it makes it more likely that group members will be interested in your products or services.

- **Offer value first.** Instead of jumping straight into a sales pitch, try to offer value to the group first. This could be in the form of a free resource, a helpful tip or advice, or even just a supportive comment. This helps to build trust and credibility, and it makes it more likely that group members will be receptive to your offers.

3. Be social. Remember that social media is about being social! Connect with other members, comment on their posts, and engage in conversations. Don't be afraid to reach out and connect with people offline as well. Don't be afraid to direct message someone and ask if you can add the person as a friend or connect if you find you have similar interests or values.

4. Be genuine. Be yourself and be authentic. People can spot a fake from a mile away, so don't try to be someone you're not. Also, don't try to be salesy or pushy. You want to know how you can connect with them first.

5. Respect the rules. Every group and community has its own set of rules, so make sure you're familiar with them before participating. For example, many groups will allow business promotion posts but maybe only once or twice a month. Not following the rules can get you banned from the group or community. I recommend reading the room, so to speak. For example, many Facebook community pages get bombarded with real estate-type promotions. If you see that, and you are in real estate, maybe try a different approach. Instead of "Hey, I have a house to sell" with photos and price—maybe avoid that and focus on interacting with people when they post garage sales. After all, sometimes a garage sale means they might be moving! Connect first—sell later—like later later!

Join the NFT Community

You're already well versed in what Web3, the metaverse, and NFTs are. So let's navigate to the real nerve center of these phenomena: the vibrant online communities.

It's often said that the best way to dive into a new digital realm is to just take the plunge! Let me help you figure out how to get started. Your first ports of call? X and Discord. Think of these platforms as the town criers of Web3 and the metaverse.

You'd be amazed at the sheer diversity of communities out there, each one buzzing with conversations and ideas. Whether you're deeply interested in the empowerment of women, or an avid follower of influential figures like Gary Vee, there's a digital community out there waiting for you.

However, a word of caution: Some communities in the Web3 and metaverse spaces can be highly exclusive, their membership limited. Persistence, patience, and open-mindedness are key as you navigate these waters.

After setting up your Discord profile, let your interests guide you. Use the search tool to find communities centered on your passions. If you're a hockey fan, there's a space for that. If music or travel piques your interest, those communities exist too. Just like social media, it takes some time to find your niche.

Here's something noteworthy: These Web3 and metaverse communities have a different feel to them. It's unlike the vague, wide-reaching attempts on platforms like Instagram to find "your people."

When you discover a project or a space within the metaverse that clicks with you, the community is part of the package. It's the difference between searching for your friends in a packed nightclub and strolling into your favorite neighborhood bar where everyone knows your name. It feels authentic, close-knit, and personal.

In summary, if you're ready to dive into the world of Web3, the metaverse, and NFTs, focus on networking and cross-promotion. Engaging with the communities is your first step. Trust me, this digital journey is an exciting one!

Cross-Promotion and Networking

When I first started podcasting and delved into NFTs, I wasn't an expert. I didn't have a community in those circles. I had to use my other social media platforms to build a community in these worlds. I would record a podcast and promote it on LinkedIn, Instagram, X, Facebook, and my website.

What began to happen is I would either host or be a guest on a podcast and I would be introduced to a new NFT project or a community. Then maybe I would be in the NFT group and talk about my podcast and see someone add me on Instagram. The flow from one to the other was organic.

That is the key! We often forget that original intent and instead focus so hard on selling ourselves, our services, or our products, that building a community or trying to gain followers seems forced. It feels like work—hard work. But if you focus on seeking out those with similar interests and organically growing your network by adding value, the business eventually comes.

Be a Go-Giver

There is another really good book titled The Go-Giver by Bob Burg and John D. Mann. It is a short business parable about the power of giving. Basically, the character of the book is ambitious and hardworking but feels he doesn't see results that match his effort. He decides to seek out The Chairman for advice and mentorship. Through the growth (abundance) mindset, he learns the Five Laws of Stratospheric Success, which are as follows:

- **Value.** Your true worth is determined by how much more you give in value than you take in payment.

- **Compensation.** Your income is determined by how many people you serve and how well you serve them.

- **Influence.** Your influence is determined by how abundantly you place other people's interests first.

- **Authenticity.** The most valuable gift you have to offer is yourself.

- **Receptivity.** The key to effective giving is to stay open to receiving.

I cannot think of any other words that sum up how to create a bond with others and build a community that people want to be a part of. If you look at each law, it sounds simple. However, in our consumer society—with all the hustle and bustle—the pressure can get to you. We have to learn to evolve from being a go-getter to a go-giver. I say, take a step back and see how you can enact the five laws.

First, when it comes to value—are you giving more than you take in compensation? And I am not talking only about the cold, hard cash. If someone offers you advice or introduces you to someone that has the potential to elevate your business, what are you doing for that person? If you have a client or customer, do you exceed expectations? Is your product or service legendary? Something a person will talk about and share with others?

When it comes to the second law of compensation, how many people do you serve? Do you serve them well? If you have worked in a sales position, you know that your number of sales gets tracked. Car sales, real estate, finance—you will see social media posts about how many deals the person does in a month, quarter, or year. But does the person ever brag about how many PEOPLE he or she has served? Is there ever a conversation about how you helped solve a complex problem for someone? Your relationships should be about quality. If the quality is there, the quantity will come.

That brings me to influence. The third law says that your influence is determined by how well you put other people's interests ahead of your own. But what does that mean? Looking back at the sales scenarios, do you sell someone a particular car because you will earn a bonus to get it off the lot? Do you convince someone to buy a particular fund or stock because it fits the person's retirement goals or because you earn a bigger commission? You gain influence by doing the right thing because it is the right thing to do.

That brings us to authenticity. I have mentioned it a few times. Be genuine. Be authentic. You are a gift. You have a natural talent, thought process, experience that is uniquely YOU. It doesn't matter if you sell the same product or service as 20 other people in your area. You have something to offer that the others do not possess. What is it? What about you is different? How are you leveraging your different point of view, perspective, products, or service? What makes you legendary?

A prime example of this was brought to me by an acquaintance. She went out to dinner with her family to a mid- to higher-end chophouse. The restaurant had an expansive and impressive wine list. However, one of the guests couldn't drink wine but wanted a beer. The beer selection was very limited, so the guest decided to stick with water. Within five minutes, the manager came to the table and asked the guest's beer preference. The manager left and returned within ten minutes with the guest's preferred beer. This establishment had a sister restaurant within a short walking distance, and the manager sent a runner to acquire the desired beer and bring it back. Do you think the other five restaurants in the area would have gone to that length to satisfy a guest? Did the restaurant do it for the sake of the sale? Of course not. It did it to create a unique and memorable experience.

The point is, you could offer the same exact service or product as someone else, but if you create an authentic and memorable experience, you set yourself over the crowd. Your social media posts are no different!

Finally, we have the law of receptivity. You have to be open to receiving! This means you must be open to the gifts of others or you stop the flow of giving. So if you struggle with accepting even a compliment, reconsider your mindset. Think about the last time someone complimented your outfit, your hair, something you said—and your response was something like, "Oh, this old thing;" or instead of saying thank you, your response was "You're crazy," or I look terrible," or "It was a lucky guess."

The key to giving is that we need givers and receivers for the flow to work, and you need to participate in a positive way. So when someone gives you a compliment, maybe respond with "Thank you, you made my day," or "Thank you, you are so kind to notice."

I know it is hard to take a compliment or gift from someone. We often feel guilty or undeserving. However, we feel good when we give, and we need to recognize that others deserve the opportunity to experience that as well. Allow others to show you acts of kindness.

The same goes when someone offers to help. Do you feel like it is a burden for the other person to help you? The person offers, and you respond with "No, it's okay. I got it. I don't want to take up your time?" When you reject the gift, the kindness, you block the flow of giving. So instead of considering acceptance as selfish, think of staying in flow.

Cross-promotion, networking, and relationship or community building are about bonding, connecting, and FLOW. Social media is one of the greatest inventions to stay in flow and practice the art of giving instead of getting!

My hope is that by now you see the value of using social media to grow relationships and build your community or find your people. I would bet your biggest hesitation is that the social media mountain seems like a big one to climb. I won't lie—if you are doing it right, it will take time and hard work in the beginning. And yes, it can be overwhelming.

But it doesn't have to be.

As the internet and social media continue to evolve, it is important for individuals and businesses to be mindful of how they are spending their time online and building their communities. In the past, the focus of many online platforms and businesses was on consumption, rather than connection and community. As a result, people became more isolated and disconnected, and the social media experience became more superficial and commercialized.

To avoid these mistakes and create more meaningful and sustainable online communities, it is important to focus on building relationships and connections with intention. This means showing up on social media and other online platforms with a clear purpose and vision and being authentic and genuine in our interactions with others.

One way to do this is by creating content and participating in online groups and communities that align with our values and interests. By doing this, we can connect with others who share similar passions and goals, creating a sense of belonging and purpose.

Another way to be more mindful of our online presence and build sustainable communities is by being more selective about the content we consume and share. Instead of simply consuming and sharing whatever is popular or trending, we can make an effort to seek out and share content that is meaningful and aligned with our values.

Finally, it is important to remember that online communities are not just about self-promotion or commercial gain. They are about building relationships, supporting one another, and creating value for all members. By showing up with intention and a give-first mentality, you will be able to have a successful social media strategy that grows your business and your network as well.

Chapter 11

What Can You Do Next?

Before we dive into the nitty-gritty of your social media journey, we must emphasize the importance of self-assessment. This segment of the chapter is dedicated to teaching you the crucial steps of auditing your social media presence. Through this process, you'll develop an understanding of your current positioning, the opportunities available to you, and the areas that need improvement.

Think of it as a self-help exercise where you play both the student and the teacher. You'll assess your social media platforms, your content, your engagement rates, and more. You'll be delving into your preferences, identifying your strengths and weaknesses, and ultimately shaping your own social media strategy.

While self-assessment is an invaluable skill and can offer you significant insights, there's also great merit in obtaining a professional's perspective. No matter how thoroughly we might assess ourselves, there are bound to be some areas we overlook simply because we're so immersed in our own businesses. That's where a professional audit, such as those provided by Next Step Social Communications, can be beneficial.

A professional audit offers a second pair of eyes that are trained to spot the things you might miss. Think of it as a safety net, providing reassurance that you're on the right track and guiding you to areas needing attention that you might not have noticed. Remember, the goal isn't to replace the self-help approach but rather to enhance it with professional guidance.

So in this chapter, we'll guide you through performing your own social media audit, setting your goals, and understanding your metrics. Once you're equipped with these skills and have put them into practice, we highly recommend supplementing your efforts with professional auditing services for that comprehensive, in-depth analysis.

Now let's start with the self-help part of your social media strategy: the audit and assessment.

You don't have to tackle everything at once—and you don't have to do it alone. There is no reason to reinvent the wheel! We are here to help with everything from brand and web design to marketing campaigns and social media consulting and management. However, if you want to tackle your social media and get it to the next level, there are some things you can do.

This chapter is a combination of a little self-help advice to get you started and some insight on what my team can do to help if you get too overwhelmed or just don't have the time to take your social media on. It's a mix of to-dos and a checklist with a safety net.

Starting a social media project with an audit or an assessment is crucial to understanding where you currently stand and where you want to go. An assessment can help you to identify your strengths, weaknesses, opportunities, and threats. It will also help you to understand your target audience and the platforms and strategies that are best suited to your business.

When conducting your assessment, consider the following questions:

- **Do you have separate social media accounts that are for business and personal use?** Having separate accounts can help you to clearly define your brand's image and make it easier to manage your content.

- **What platforms are you currently using?** Knowing which platforms you are using will help you to understand where the people in your audience are and how you can reach them.

- **Do you have a favorite platform?** And is that where you see the most engagement? Identifying your favorite platform will help you to understand which platform you are most comfortable using and where you are seeing the most engagement. It can also help you to understand which platform will be the most beneficial for your business.

Additionally, you can also analyze your competitors and see what kind of social media presence they have and what is working for them. By conducting a thorough assessment, you'll be able to make a well-informed decision about your social media strategy. Having a clear understanding of where you are and where you want to go is the first step in developing a successful social media plan.

Identifying your social media goals is an important step in creating a successful social media strategy. It allows you to focus your efforts and track your progress toward achieving specific objectives. Here are some common social media goals that businesses may want to achieve:

- **Increase brand awareness.** This goal is about getting your brand in front of as many people as possible. This can be achieved by creating high-quality, engaging content and actively engaging with your audience. Building a strong presence on social media can help to increase awareness of your brand and improve brand recall.

- **Engage with customers/build relationships.** Building strong relationships with your customers is key to long-term success. This goal focuses on fostering engagement with people by creating content that resonates with them and responding to comments, messages, and reviews in a timely manner. This type of engagement helps to build trust and loyalty among your customers.

- **Drive traffic to your website.** Increasing website traffic is a common goal for businesses, as it can help to drive leads and sales. Social media can be a powerful tool to drive traffic to your website, by sharing links to your content and promoting your products and services.

- **Generate leads/sales conversions.** Social media is a great way to generate leads and increase conversions. By providing value-adding content, offering discounts and promotions, and actively engaging with your audience, you can convert your followers into customers.

- **Improve customer service.** Social media can also be an effective tool for providing customer service. By monitoring social media for mentions of your brand and responding promptly to customer inquiries, you can improve your customer service and build stronger relationships with your audience.

Once you have identified your social media goals, it's important to take an in-depth look at your current social media presence to understand how you can improve it. By conducting a social media audit, you'll be able to identify what is working well, what needs improvement, and where you can make changes to achieve your goals.

When doing an audit, you should consider the following questions for each platform:

- **How often am I posting?** This will help you to understand if you are posting frequently enough to maintain your audience's engagement and stay top of mind.

- **What type of content am I posting?** This will help you to understand if your content is aligned with your goals and resonating with your audience.

- **Is my content engaging?** This will help you to understand if your content is generating engagement and interaction from your audience.

- **Who is my audience?** This will help you to understand who is following you, what demographics are interested in your content, and what kind of content your audience likes to see.

- **How am I attracting new followers/fans?** This will help you to understand how you are reaching new audiences and what strategies are working best to attract new followers.

- **How many people are visiting my profile each week?** This will help you to understand how much traffic you are getting to your profile and how you can improve your visibility.

Additionally, you can also compare your social media metrics with industry benchmarks and your competitors' metrics—which can give you a good perspective on how you are performing compared with others. This can help you to identify areas where you need to improve and give you ideas for how to grow your following and engagement. Overall, conducting a social media audit can help you to identify opportunities to improve your social media presence and achieve your goals. If you need assistance conducting a social media audit, we would love to help. You can book a social media audit with Next Step Social Communications at nextstepsocial.as.me/audit.

Once you have a good understanding of where you stand, you can start to put together a plan to improve your social media presence. This is where the data from your audit comes in handy. Use it to determine what's working and what's not. From there, you can start to develop a content strategy that will help you achieve your social media goals.

Remember that each platform has some analytics capabilities. but to really get the big picture, you might need to invest in some of the tools discussed earlier.

Build a Content Strategy

We touched on content strategy earlier, but this is the meat and bones. Your content strategy should be rooted in your goals. What do you want to achieve? How can you use content to get there? There are also some useful tips to consider. For example, the goal is to educate, enlighten, or entertain.

When developing your content strategy, it's important to appeal to different interests and preferences within your audience. Some people may be drawn to logical content focused on data, facts, and practical information. Others may be more compelled by creative content that stirs emotions through storytelling, humor, or visuals.

To connect with the full spectrum of your followers, aim for variety in your social media content. Share informative articles, how-to tutorials, entertaining videos, inspiring quotes, and engaging stories. Appeal to those who love science and math, and also those who appreciate comedy and art.

Remember, your social media should ultimately be geared toward building community and fostering two-way engagement. To achieve this, tailor your content to resonate across personalities and learning styles. Experiment to see which topics and formats your audience most closely connects with.

The key is understanding that people consume content differently.

Keep your messaging aligned with your brand voice while diversifying the types of posts. This thoughtful mix will allow you to effectively engage the widest range of people possible on social platforms.

Here are some content ideas that can help you get started:

- **Blog posts.** These are great for providing information and inspiration to your audience. You can write about different topics related to your industry, share tips and insights, or share stories about your business. Mixing up your blog post topics will keep your audience engaged and coming back for more.

- **Videos.** Videos are a great way to connect with your audience. Mix up your video content with a combination of how-to tutorials, industry news, and even funny videos to add a personal touch.

- **Infographics.** Infographics are a great way to present information in an easy-to-digest format. Use them to share statistics, facts, and data that your audience will find valuable, but don't be afraid to add a touch of humor or levity to make them more engaging.

- **How-to guides.** These are great for both logical and creative learners. They can provide value to your audience by teaching them new skills and techniques.

- **Case studies.** Case studies are a great way to share real-world examples of how your products or services have helped your customers. Don't be afraid to get creative with your case studies; there are endless possibilities of examples.

- **Whitepapers/e-books.** These are great for providing more in-depth information and insights on specific topics. You don't have to make them boring; you can add some visual elements— including infographics—to make them more engaging.

- **Industry news.** Keep your audience informed about the latest developments in your industry by sharing news, bloopers, and fun facts.

- **Images.** Keep images professional and on topic. Consider current trends, and use them as much as possible, as that can also grab the attention of your audience.

Keep in mind, it's important to not just focus on one content type, but to mix and match, test and evaluate what resonates well with your audience, and make changes accordingly.

In addition to creating a variety of engaging content, it's also important to include calls to action (CTAs) in every piece of content you create. CTAs are a way of guiding your audience toward taking a specific action after consuming your content. The purpose of a CTA is to convert leads into customers by encouraging them to take the next step.

There are many different types of CTAs that you can use, depending on the type of content you're creating and the action you want your audience to take. Some examples of CTAs include:

- **Asking your audience to like, share, save, or comment on the post.** This helps to increase the visibility and reach of your content and fosters engagement with your community.

- **Directing your audience to your website or blog.** This can help to drive traffic to your site, where you can further engage with your audience and convert leads into customers.

- **Encouraging your audience to sign up for your newsletter.** This can help you to build a list of engaged subscribers who are interested in your products or services.

- **Asking your audience to download a whitepaper or e-book.** This can help you to generate leads and build relationships with the people in your audience by providing them with valuable information.

When crafting CTAs, make sure they are clear, action-oriented, and easy to understand. Make them visually stand out in your content, and be specific about the next step you want your audience to take. For example, instead of saying "Learn more," use "Download our whitepaper;" it will be more specific. Additionally, make sure that the CTA is relevant to the content and that the link or button people are clicking on leads to the appropriate page or action.

In conclusion, incorporating calls to action into your content is an important step in converting leads into customers. By providing clear, action-oriented CTAs, you can guide the people in your audience toward taking the next step in their journey with your business.

When it comes to creating high-quality, engaging content, it's important to keep the people in your audience in mind. The content you create should be valuable and helpful to them, not just a means to an end for you. Take the time to research their needs, wants, and interests and create content that speaks to them. This can include blog posts, videos, infographics, how-to guides, case studies, whitepapers, e-books, industry news, and images that inform, educate, and entertain your audience.

In addition to creating high-quality content, it's also important to be consistent with your posting. Posting a few times and then going silent will not help you achieve your goals. Consistency is key to building a loyal audience, and creating a steady stream of content will help you maintain your audience's attention. A content calendar can be a helpful tool to plan and organize your content, so you can ensure that you're posting on a regular basis.

It's essential to not just post, but also actively engage with your audience, respond to comments, answer questions, and participate in online conversations. This will help to foster a sense of community around your brand and make your audience feel valued.

It's also important to analyze and measure the performance of your content, to understand how it's impacting your audience and your business. This will help you to make data-driven decisions on what works and what doesn't, and make any necessary adjustments to your content strategy.

Remember, creating high-quality, helpful content is an essential part of building a strong social media presence and achieving your business goals. Consistency in creating and distributing your content, along with audience engagement and measurement, is crucial to your success in this field.

Build a Content Calendar

Consistency means having a regimented schedule. If you don't schedule it, there is a greater likelihood it won't happen. Once you have a good idea of the content you want to share, you need to build a content calendar to help keep you consistent. A content calendar helps keep your variety of posts in rotation and the calendar can auto-post for you, so you are posting when people are on the platforms. This is important because you want your content to be seen by as many people as possible.

To get started, map out when you are going to post which type of content. For example, are Motivation Monday and Throwback Thursday in the cards? Then start filling in the calendar with specific posts. Maybe Monday will be images and inspirational quotes, and Thursday can be history or historical facts about your industry ("On this day" posts).

Remember, you don't have to reinvent the wheel. There are content calendar templates out there. You can get one free by visiting www. katiebrinkley.com/contentcalendar.

The Tools

Now you need to make a list of the tools you need and get them together and ready to go. Here is a quick rundown to get you started:

- Social media accounts separate from your personal accounts

- List of goals to keep your eye on the ball

- Analytical tools to track engagement, what is working, what isn't

- Content calendar to organize and post content

- Content that is engaging

- Time blocked on the calendar to review analytics, create content, and make changes

Lastly, if you've given it your best shot but something isn't clicking, or you find yourself feeling frustrated or overwhelmed—remember, it's perfectly okay to call in the experts. Social media has its complexities, and the landscape is ever-changing. Managing it on top of your regular duties, family, and social life can be a daunting task. Recognizing when you need a helping hand is a mark of wisdom, not defeat.

When you do decide to reach out to a professional, look for someone with proven experience and an understanding of your unique business needs. The person should be up-to-date with the latest trends and changes in social media, be able to guide you on the best platforms for your business, and have the skills to create engaging content that resonates with your target audience. A good expert can help you navigate the challenges, optimize your efforts, and take your social media presence to new heights. It's not just about easing the workload—it's about making your social media efforts as effective as possible.

It's About Service

I want to help. First, through this book. I want to provide value and know that when I give freely, I open myself up to receiving. Maybe I receive a social media management engagement—or maybe—and more importantly—I receive friendship and build community through being a connector. Either way, I want to help where I can.

My company, Next Step Social Communications, specializes in social media communications. We offer a full suite of services to help our clients connect with their audiences in the most effective way possible. If you are overwhelmed, we offer:

- **Social media consulting.** We will work with you to develop a social media strategy that meets your specific goals and objectives. We can even help do social media account audits to see what is working (or not) on your accounts. We can advise on creating your social media voice, the best hashtags to use, and more!

- **Social media management.** If you don't have the time or don't want to, we will manage your social media accounts for you, posting content, engaging with followers, and monitoring activity. We will analyze your accounts and posts to make sure they are optimized for engagement and community building. We set your social media content calendar with posts that educate, enlighten, or entertain—hitting on both the logical and creative way of thinking!

- **Social media advertising.** We can help you create and implement effective social media advertising campaigns that reach your target audience. Have you tried a Facebook ad and it proved to be a waste of your time and money? We can fix that! Each platform is a little different, and we know what works and what doesn't. We also keep up with all the changes, so you don't have to.

- **Web design and development.** We offer custom web design and development services that will help you build an online presence that truly reflects your brand. Your social media and website should be consistent. This is the face of your business, and you need to be easily recognized. Colors, fonts, and layout speak volumes. We can help bring your personality and style together so everything is cohesive and functional.

- **Branding.** Do you have a brand strategy? Does your competition? Do you know what a brand strategy is? We can help you develop and implement a brand strategy that will make you stand out from the competition. We are like the interior designers of your business. We take color, fonts, themes, and logo design to build your business story.

- **Marketing services.** We offer a wide range of marketing services, from traditional advertising to cutting-edge digital marketing campaigns. Have an event and want a marketing campaign leading up to the day? We can help! Do you need a creative email drip campaign to build a contact list? We can help do that too!

My business philosophy is about nurturing a genuine relationship between you and your audience. I like to think I walk the walk. Our social media content isn't canned and scripted for sales. My team takes the time to listen and develop a custom plan that works for you and your business. Big or small, we want your audience to feel welcome. Your social media should be inviting and engaging. We want your audience to share, like, and, most of all, interact with you and your business. That is the goal!

It's About Time

I think the greatest gift my team gives is the gift of time. My team and I have worked for many clients to improve their social media and branding. One of the key benefits of working with us is that we give you your time back. We can take the burden of social media off your hands, so that you have time to spend with family or to work on or in your business. One of my proudest moments was getting this testimonial from my client Kim at Home Method Co.:

> *"Next Step Social Communications is amazing! I recently re-branded and re-launched my Home Organization business. For 10 years I have dreamed of hiring someone to take over my social media. As a full-time working mom of 2 kids and business owner, the only time I had to catch up on social media was late at night. Now after working with Next Step Social Communications, I can focus on running my business and being more present with my family. Next Step Social Communications has changed my life! I would recommend them to anyone!"*

Not only do we strive to give you time back through social media management, but we do the research so you don't have to. Social media and branding are our business. We stay on top of all the platform changes, algorithms, and best practices. Think about it—how many social media accounts do you currently have? Two? Five? More? Then think about the upgrades, updates, and changes each platform makes. And then think about how many times you thought you got in a rhythm, and it changes again, or the platform tweaks the algorithm or adds a new feature. It can be enough to make your head spin—or make you want to give up. It's enough to try to keep up with computer and phone updates!

It's About Knowledge and Experience

I also like to think that I give my clients the gift of sharing my knowledge and experience. I've been tracking and using the platforms since the beginning. I have a solid foundation of knowledge when it comes to how things work and what used to work versus how they are now. It might not seem like much to some, but that foundational knowledge gives me (and you) an advantage. I use it to track what might come next or how to optimize what just came out. I have a vision of ideas, techniques, and proven processes that are efficient.

We also know the tools of the trade, so to speak. If it's not enough to keep up with the platforms, now think about learning the tools to use so that you are hitting your goals. Your time is worth money. So how much money (time) are you willing to burn to learn the different social media tools? How long do you want to spend researching and analyzing hashtags? Of course, if you are a MAVEN, you might be enthusiastic. But if you want to be a CONNECTOR, your time is better spent talking to people rather than huddling over analytics.

If you have decided that you are ready to commit but don't have the time or patience to do it on your own, our process is pretty straightforward.

Our Process

We offer an easy and friendly way to learn more about how we can help. First, we will do a phone interview with you to discover what your marketing needs are and how we can fill the gaps. Our call is detailed, and you will get a custom marketing plan based on your goals. We even offer weekly or monthly service options. If you decide you want to move forward from there, we will begin the execution of the marketing plan based on the agreed terms. It could be a full turnkey engagement, from providing simple social media management to creating a brand strategy all the way through content creation, posting, and ad campaigns.

No matter what options you choose, when we execute the digital marketing solution, it will bring your online presence to life! You will see in full color and real time how things will look. We check in to make sure you approve of the details. Then it's all about maintenance.

We provide weekly and monthly reporting options to monitor growth and progress. You will see the results of ad campaigns, post engagement, and growth in followers. We will adjust to make sure we meet your milestones and conquer any hurdles along the way.

Final Thoughts

In the uncharted cosmos of the digital age, we're passengers on a journey driven by relentless technological evolution. With each passing moment, this evolution reshapes the landscape, setting up novel challenges and offering enticing opportunities to revive a fundamental aspect of human life—community. From the era of the telegraph and radio to the thrilling emergence of Web3 and metaverse technologies, an essential survival skill has been our capacity to adapt and adopt, else we risk being left behind.

As of 2023, the number of social media users worldwide exceeds 4.5 billion. This staggering figure is a testament to the all-pervasive influence of these platforms. Experts project that by 2027, this number will soar to an astounding 6 billion. Dominating the social media arena are Facebook, YouTube, Instagram, and TikTok—the last of which saw an unprecedented 142 percent year-over-year increase in 2021. And now as we venture into the era of NFTs and Web3, platforms such as Reddit have seen a significant spike in user engagement, a testament to the continued expansion and evolution of the digital landscape.

Consider the elders in your life—perhaps your grandparents or even great-grandparents if they are still around. They have witnessed immense technological transformations over the decades, from the rise of telephones, radio and TV to the digital revolution.

Throughout all this change, they've adapted and found value in each new advancement, even if initially foreign or challenging. Their resilience and openness to evolve with the times serves as an inspirational model.

Now as we venture into emerging realms like artificial intelligence, blockchain and the metaverse, we can draw wisdom from their approach. Major shifts can be daunting, yet giving new innovations a chance often unveils opportunity. Rather than recoiling, lean in with an experimental mindset.

Each generation faces its own technological frontiers. The elders in our lives have modeled courage and flexibility amidst uncertainty. As our digital landscape continues advancing, we can honor our predecessors by embracing this spirit of openness.

Some have even welcomed smartphones into their lives, primarily to stay connected with younger generations. They push against the fear of missing out, seeking relevance and connection—an instinct inherent in all of us. Their experiences underscore the absolute necessity of social media and technology in our lives today.

Since the dawn of human civilization, community has been the cornerstone that holds society together. It's the familiar thread that weaves individuals into the fabric of a shared existence, fostering a sense of security, belonging, and trust.

Community is how we share information, news, and events and how we socially interact. Without that sense of belonging, we become isolated and vulnerable. Community is an essential part of health and happiness.

The Robert Wood Johnson Foundation found that "individuals who feel a sense of security, belonging, and trust in their community have better health. People who don't feel connected are less inclined to act in healthy ways or work with others to promote well-being for all." By using social media as a CONNECTOR, you could be improving and promoting the health and well-being of your followers. Think about how powerful this is!

One of the profound aspects of the digital age is its ability to dissolve geographical boundaries and cultural barriers. The internet, and more specifically, social media, has given us the unparalleled power to find "our people," our community, no matter where we are. It has birthed a new kind of global village where shared interests, values, and aspirations bind people more strongly than geographical proximity ever could. You could be in New York and find kinship with someone in Tokyo, all because of a shared love for abstract art, sustainability, or a particular genre of music. This openness is not just about breaking physical boundaries—it also allows us to shatter the limitations of our understanding, fostering a sense of inclusivity and acceptance. When you venture into the digital realm, you're not just a passive consumer— you're an active participant in shaping and defining these communities. By taking the plunge and being open to connections, you might just find a tribe that not only understands and accepts you for who you are, but also inspires you to grow and evolve.

A study from Deloitte in 2019 found that in higher education, students' sense of belonging is associated with retention. In the workplace, Deloitte reported that "belonging, along with well-being, is at the top of the Global Human Capital Trends survey," with almost 80 percent of the respondents answering that fostering a sense of belonging was important. From small businesses to Fortune 100s, creating community is at the forefront. From surveys to studies, it is clear that a sense of community—this sense of belonging—leads to better performance, health, and happiness.

It's undeniable that social media poses challenges such as cyberbullying, body image issues, and political polarization. However, these platforms are not inherently malevolent. The power of social media can be harnessed for positive change, for strengthening our connections and fostering resilient networks. The emerging technologies of Web3. and the metaverse represent the extension of this potential, offering rich, immersive interactions and the possibility of even closer community ties.

As we meander toward the finale of our social media journey, it feels fitting to revisit the four-post strategy, that trusty blueprint unveiled a few chapters back. This proven approach offers clarity amid the dizzying array of platforms and choices, providing a road map to engage your audience while retaining sanity.

The four-post formula leverages the awareness-to-action continuum to move your audience smoothly through the conversion funnel. No more aimless posting or content fatigue. Just a sustainable cadence designed to captivate and convert.

By blending informative, helpful, promotional, and community-focused content in batches, you increase engagement and achieve results efficiently. The framework adapts seamlessly across platforms while retaining core principles:

- Creating relevant content aligned with audience interests

- Maintaining consistent messaging and visuals for brand recognition

- Increasing educational value with each installment

- Incorporating calls to action appropriately to avoid a salesy vibe

For example, an effective four-post Instagram batch could include:

1. An attention-grabbing Reel with an intriguing statistic

2. A tip post elaborating on an actionable strategy from the reel

3. A behind-the-scenes Instagram Story peek into your business

4. A product post with a swipe-up link to your online shop

This mini-narrative nurtures the audience through the purchase journey. The educational and community posts earn you the right to incorporate organic call-to-action driving conversions.

Similarly, the four-post blueprint can be applied across other platforms like Facebook, LinkedIn, and Instagram using ideal formats tailored to each. The framework remains consistent while the content presentation aligns with the platform.

Continually analyze metrics like reach, engagement, traffic, and conversions to optimize your efforts over time. Let the data reveal what resonates so you can refine each four-post batch.

Adopting the four-post strategy equips you with an adaptable framework optimized for today's fractured digital landscape. As we journey into emerging technologies like the metaverse, this approach will continue providing clarity.

The future may bring new modes of connection, but compelling storytelling endures. By focusing on educational value and community building, you earn the right to incorporate promotion and calls to action. The four-post content blueprint strikes this delicate balance successfully.

In a social media sphere pushing for more posts, remember—less can truly be more. Embrace the four-post method to maximize your impact while maintaining sanity. Consistency, restraint, and added value—this is the pathway forward.

As our digital landscape advances with innovations like Web3 and the metaverse, adapting to these new platforms will be instrumental. But to truly thrive as a connector, start with strengthening your presence on current platforms.

Step by step, expand your digital literacy. This experience prepares you not just to exist in the future, but to help shape it. Appreciate technology's potential to foster connections. Know that your efforts, no matter how small, bring us closer to a global community.

The digital world is no longer the future—it's the present. Embrace the opportunities this journey offers. While challenging at times, the rewards make it worthwhile.

Stay curious; stay connected. With an innovative mindset, you will dive into the digital universe and emerge with stronger, more meaningful bonds that enrich our lives.

To truly thrive as a connector in this rapidly evolving digital world, you need to start with the present—our existing platforms. Step by step, as you broaden your understanding and expand your digital literacy, you're preparing not just to exist in the future, but to influence it actively.

Remember, technology is merely a tool—it's how we wield it that shapes our world. By leveraging social media and digital platforms to foster connection, we're contributing to a more cohesive, inclusive global community. No matter how daunting the journey may seem, know that every effort is a step toward a more interconnected world.

As you forge ahead, always keep the power of community in mind. Appreciate the potential of technology to foster deeper, more meaningful connections. In this exploration, you're not just preparing yourself for the future—you're shaping it. And with every small step you take toward understanding this digital realm, you're making a giant leap toward building a more connected, inclusive community.

Stay curious, stay connected, and remember—the digital world is no longer the future; it's the present. So take the plunge, and embrace the opportunities it offers. The journey may be challenging, but the rewards are worth every effort. Dive in—the digital universe awaits you.

About the Author

Katie Brinkley is the founder and lead strategist of Next Step Social Communications, a digital marketing agency based in Littleton, Colorado.

Driven by a passion for helping businesses grow through the strategic use of social media and online platforms, Katie founded Next Step Social Communications in 2017. Under her leadership, the agency empowers brands to effectively connect with their target audiences and thrive in the digital space.

Katie's fascination with social media strategy began early in her career. In the early 2000s, she helped local bands build their fanbase and promote their music through customized MySpace pages. This hands-on experience showed her the power of strategic social media marketing for audience growth and community engagement.

She later drew on over a decade of experience in radio, digital media, and marketing. She previously worked as an on-air talent and postgame reporter for Denver's 850 KOA radio station. During this time, she gained firsthand insight into developing engaging content, building an audience, and leveraging multimedia platforms.

Prior to starting her agency, Katie served as Marketing Manager for DirecTV Sports Network. In this role, she oversaw marketing campaigns and partnerships for regional sports networks. Her successes included increasing social media engagement and website traffic through compelling content and strategic promotions.

Her background in radio sparked Katie's fascination with podcasting. In 2020, she took the leap into podcast hosting and quickly saw its power for generating leads and establishing thought leadership. This hands-on experience fuels Katie's commitment to helping clients maximize emerging digital platforms.

At Next Step Social Communications, Katie oversees a talented team that provides services ranging from social media consulting and management to blogging, branding, and marketing campaigns. With an emphasis on authentic engagement and measurable growth, the agency crafts custom strategies tailored to each client's brand, goals, and target audience.

When she isn't advising clients, Katie stays active in the digital marketing community. She frequently hosts workshops and speaks on using social media and podcasting to accelerate business growth. Katie also shares regular insights through her own podcast, Rocky Mountain Marketing, and social channels.

With over two decades specializing in digital communication, Katie is passionate about keeping brands ahead of the curve. She constantly tracks emerging social media trends and equips clients with the latest tools to thrive. Katie's hands-on guidance empowers brands to harness the power of strategic content to engage meaningfully and drive real results.

Contact Us

—————

If you want to learn more about Next Step Social Communications, you can find us at www.NextStepSocialCommunications.com

On the web: www.nextstepsocialcommunications.com

On Facebook: www.facebook.com/iamkatiebrinkley

On Instagram: https://www.instagram.com/iamkatiebrinkley/

On LinkedIn : https://www.linkedin.com/in/katiebrinkley/

Want to learn more about social media, sales, and marketing? Listen to Katie's podcast *Rocky Mountain Marketing Podcast* at https://www. nextstepsocialcommunications.com/podcast.

www.ingramcontent.com/pod-product-compliance
Lightning Source LLC
La Vergne TN
LVHW051334050326
832903LV00031B/3542